My First Introduction to the New Testament

My First Introduction to the New Testament

Sharon R. Chace

RESOURCE *Publications* · Eugene, Oregon

My First Introduction to the New Testament

Copyright © 2011 Sharon R. Chace. All rights reserved. Except for brief quotations in critical publications or reviews, no part of this book may be reproduced in any manner without prior written permission from the publisher. Write: Permissions, Wipf and Stock Publishers, 199 W. 8th Ave., Suite 3, Eugene, OR 97401.

All Scripture quotations are taken from the New Revised Standard Version Bible, copyright 1989, Division of Christian Education of the National Council of the Churches of Christ in the United States of America. Used by permission. All rights reserved.

Resource Publications
An Imprint of Wipf and Stock Publishers
199 W. 8th Ave., Suite 3
Eugene, OR 97401

www.wipfandstock.com

ISBN 13: 978-1-60899-821-0

Manufactured in the U.S.A.

Dedicated to Rosemary Lesch,
Sister of heart and hearth,
Friend, whose work is very different from mine,
yet understands that my work is real work,
Harbormaster, who has helped me navigate
stormy challenges.

Contents

Foreword by Harry T. Cook   ix
Author's Letter to Young Readers   xiii

1. What Is the New Testament?   1
2. Looking at the New Testament Like an Artist   5
3. The Basic Story of Jesus's Life   8

Part 1: The Story of Jesus and How It Spread

4. The Gospel according to Mark   13
5. The Gospel according to Matthew   19
6. The Gospel according to Luke   24
7. The Acts of the Apostles   30

Part 2: John and His Community of Loving Friends

8. The Gospel according to John   39
9. The Letters of First, Second, and Third John   48

Part 3: Paul and His Writing Friends

10. Introducing Paul   55
11. The First and Second Letters to the Thessalonians   57
12. The Letter to the Ephesians   61

Part 4: The Rest of Paul's Letters
- 13 The Letter to the Galatians 67
- 14 The First Letter to the Corinthians 70
- 15 The Second Letter to the Corinthians 76
- 16 The Letter to the Romans 81
- 17 The Letter to Philemon 90
- 18 The Letter to the Philippians 93

Part 5: Christ Served by Growing Ministry
- 19 The Letter to the Colossians 101
- 20 The Letter of James 105
- 21 The First and Second Letters to Timothy, and the Letter to Titus 110

Part 6: Christians in Trouble
- 22 The First Letter of Peter 119
- 23 The Letter of Jude 122
- 24 The Second Letter of Peter 124

Part 7: Jesus as Helper, and Christ as the Risen Lord
- 25 The Letter to the Hebrews 129
- 26 The Book of Revelation 136

Chart of New Testament Lenses 149
Author's Letter to Teachers 151
For Further Study 153

Foreword

ALL TOO INFREQUENTLY, A believer—a person of faith—will take pen to hand and write about the Bible or some part of it with considerable scholarship as background but with the immediate goal of teaching the uninitiated without (a) putting them to sleep or (b) putting them off.

Conversely, how often have we whose lifetime scholarly interests have been in translating, analyzing, and interpreting biblical texts become lost in a welter of footnotes and qualifications of this tense or that, in competing translations of Hebrew or Greek words—proudly setting down the result of our labors as major contributions to knowledge. Well, they may be, but your city's telephone directory is also a contribution to the knowledge of, say, the number and location of the nearest auto repair garage. Such knowledge is rightly deemed useful.

Another way for believers to write about the Bible is in that imperious way so many have; i.e., this is the Word of the only God there is, so pay attention. Hard-core, hard-edged evangelism, in other words.

Sharon Chace's *My First Introduction to the New Testament* will put no one but the terminal narcoleptic to sleep and certainly not put off any interested inquirer who may not, in fact, wish to become a believer but, rather, will want simply to know what all the fuss is about this thing called "the New Testament."

"Useful" is one adjective that will come to mind as the reader leafs through, then digs into this book—useful, as in introducing the history, provenance, and content of the New Testament to adult seekers either for their own edification or to equip them to teach it to fellow adults or to teenaged Sunday school students.

"Accessible" it is as well. Without talking down to her readers, Chace will be found in serious but not stilted conversation with them. She writes most often in simple declarative sentences, a rarity among many of us who deal in allegedly more academic ways with biblical texts. Chace employs mention of color and texture—terms and concepts she used with remarkable success in her previous book *An Artistic Approach to New Testament Literature*.

The reader will smile at first when he or she encounters Chace's depiction of the author of Mark wearing "dark sun glasses" while Luke's are "rose-colored." Eventually, the reader will nod and smile again, having seen, with Chace's help, the important differences between the two gospels.

When Chace discusses the setting apart of deacons depicted in the Acts of the Apostles she writes: "Church administrators are picked to run the church's meal program." Who can't grasp that?

Of John 3:16 she writes: "Another interpretation [of the verse] is that people who believe in Jesus's ethic of service, compassion, and forgiveness will be part of an ongoing movement that will matter forever." No snide disabusing of the ignorant or the orthodox here, just a gentle suggestion that salvation may have to do as much with ordinary acts of mercy and kindness as with abstract theology.

Here's how you will see her deal with one of the major differences between the Synoptic Gospels and the Gospel according to John: "People do not talk in normal conversations like Jesus talks in John. So the style of Jesus's speech is a big hint that this gospel is a *theological* document." Chace pretty much thinks the Synoptics are to a greater degree reportage.

This book is an important contribution to a cause that sometimes seems well-nigh hopeless. I speak of "biblical literacy." Not that teaching the Bible need be thought of as a matter of evangelism and conversion, though it sometimes is. The enjoyment and understanding of so much of classic English and American literature is impossible for those who have not attained at least an elementary acquaintance with the Bible. Try to understand almost any line of *Paradise Lost* and many allusions in the plays of William Shakespeare, even the priceless treasures that are the speeches of Abraham Lincoln, without knowing something of the biblical text. Language lurking among laws and statutes and in the clauses of insurance policies mentions the "good Samaritan." Much social critique references the "prodigal son." And it wasn't your Great Aunt Matilda who first said, "Pride goeth before a fall."

Chace knows all that. She obviously loves the texts of the New Testament and is well versed in their form and content. Her book will be a boon to many a busy parish minister, distracted Christian education director, and harried Sunday school superintendent.

Will it satisfy one who has made an idol of the Bible and insists that its contents are meant only to be read, marked, and inwardly digested as holy writ rather than to be investigated as to provenance, authorship, and place in history? No, it will not. And for that reason alone—among many reasons—*My First Introduction to the New Testament* is a welcome addition to the library of biblical studies.

The pedagogy recommended in its pages is enlightened and, as I have said, useful and accessible. When you turn over this page, you will find yourself in a very inviting and informative space. Even if you think you know a lot about the New Testament, Chace, as gallery docent, will point out light and shadow that may have escaped even the most erudite in their scholarly scrutiny of the text. Thanks to Chace, the non-scholar will be delighted and charmed by what a treasure the New Testament text is.

Harry T. Cook

Author's Letter to Young Readers

DEAR YOUNG READERS,
Thank you for your curiosity about the New Testament, how it came to be, and how to enjoy looking at it like an artist.

The purpose of this letter is to tell you a little about myself and why I wrote this book. As I write this letter to you, I am sixty-six years old, and that is old enough to be your grandmother or great-grandmother. I have been interested in the Bible since my Sunday school days. My family did not have a car until I was about twelve years old. So I went to whatever Sunday school was in walking distance. At first I went to Sunday school at the Universalist Church in Rockport, Massachusetts, but when we moved to Pigeon Cove, which is the north village of Rockport, I went to an evangelical church called the Pigeon Cove Chapel. Even as an eight-year-old, I knew that these two churches were very different, but leaders in both churches taught that we are all God's children and loved equally by God. That was certainly good news to me, the clumsy kickball player, who kicked the ball after it was in the catcher's hands. In sympathy, my classmates tried to figure out how to adapt our playground games, which did not work too well. But their efforts were what really mattered. I suspected that my classmates learned to care at their various churches. I also knew that the idea that God loves all people came from the Bible and concluded that the Bible is a very important book.

In 1954, as a reward for memorizing many Bible passages, I received my King James Bible from the Pigeon Cove Chapel. I had many questions. For example, are the words of Jesus that are in red really his exact words? Or are the red words like extra quotation marks? My teachers were certain that they are his exact words, but I was not sure. In time, I majored in art and minored in English and religion at Albion College in Albion, Michigan. Over thirty years later in 1998, I received a master of theological studies degree with a biblical concentration from Weston Jesuit School of Theology in Cambridge, Massachusetts. The school has now moved to Boston College and is called the School of Theology and Ministry. In my college and graduate school days, I learned that the biblical authors, like other authors in their time, would put a few words into the mouths of people that the authors thought they could have and perhaps should have said. The biblical writers were not newspaper reporters. They were more like artists. The New Testament authors used their writing skills to tell us about Jesus, his way, and how the gospel message of God's gift of Jesus spread throughout the ancient world. The Bible still speaks today. Because I am an artist and a poet, I value the artistry of the biblical writers.

In this book we will look at the story of Jesus and how this story is told in slightly different ways. We will also explore the letters of Paul to see how he helped churches grow in size, Christian love, and service. This book is the one I wished I had when I was young. You may read it on your own or a teacher might read it to you in a class. When you are older you may want to read my book *An Artistic Approach to New Testament Literature*, which is the adult version of this book. At the very end of this book, there is a letter for your teachers with suggestions for using both books. Who knows? Perhaps in several years, you, my young readers, will use my books in teaching.

For now, let us be on our way as we journey together through the New Testament. In chapter 1, I will briefly describe the New Testament and how it came to be. In chapter 2, I explain more about what it means to look at the New Testament like an artist. Come let us see together.

Sincerely,

Sharon R. Chace

Rockport, Massachusetts

Summer, 2010

1

What Is the New Testament?

The New Testament is a collection of twenty-seven books containing many different kinds of writing. New Testament authors recorded the life, death, crucifixion, and, in Christian belief, the resurrection of Jesus. Stories and letters about the spread of Jesus's message, problems in the early churches, and the development of the early church are also part of the New Testament.

The New Testament is also the second and shorter part of the Bible. The first section is called the *Old Testament* or the *Hebrew Scriptures*. In our society, the word *new* often implies the word *better*. However, the word *new* can also imply *updated* or *broadened*. The Old Testament records the Hebrews' life of faith in their one God. By telling the story of Jesus, the New Testament opens up belief in one fair and forgiving God to everyone. Therefore, the New Testament broadens and updates the story of God's steadfast love. Christians believe that Jesus shows us what God is like and how God wants people to live.

During the first third of the first century, Jesus lived, healed, and taught love of neighbor and God's forgiveness through ethical sayings that model how people should forgive one another. In the second third plus a few more years, people spread his teachings by word of mouth. Telling the stories before they were recorded is called *oral tradition*. Paul started some of his writing in this middle stage. Then, in the last third of the first century, when most of the writing was done, more people wrote down the sayings of Jesus, recorded how the story of Jesus spread, explained what Jesus meant to them, and told about life in the early church.

Authors in Jesus's time followed writing guidelines that were flexible. They were not news reporters like our newspaper writers today. Thus they felt free to put a few words into the mouths of people that these people could have said. As artistic writers, the New Testament authors explained what Jesus meant to them and how they followed him. These writers conveyed what they knew to be true about Jesus and his way. Like people today, they wrote in a form that best suited their purposes. For example, if your family goes to the grocery store, you make a list of groceries. If you have an interesting tale to tell, you write a story. If you want to tell a friend who lives in another city or town or city about your activities, you write a letter, e-mail, or text message. Choosing the kind of writing that best conveyed their messages, the writers of the New Testament gave us the story of Jesus and how early Christianity spread throughout the ancient world.

There are many kinds of writing in the New Testament. There are short sayings of Jesus and long letters from Paul to the churches. There are poems and prayers. Lists of ancestors and stories of Jesus's birth, life, and death are all part of the New Testament. Jesus told a very artistic story called a *parable*. Parables are stories that help people think about the meanings of the stories by comparing something ordinary, such as baking bread, to something extraordinary, such as the kingdom of God or how to use our talents. Sometimes the kingdom of God is called *God's reign*.

The official list of books included in the New Testament is called the *canon*. This list was not decided upon quickly. The books that were chosen were helpful to the community, in agreement with the basic beliefs of the early church, and associated in some ways with the apostles who were the first followers of Jesus. The word *canon* can also mean "ruler" or "the way we measure the ways we live." The Bible is a core document to guide anyone who chooses to read it.

The following activities will help you remember how the New Testament came to be.

ACTIVITIES

Forms of Writing in the New Testament

Take a piece of computer or construction paper to represent the entire New Testament. Then cut or tear pieces of construction paper into small pieces and write the different kinds of biblical writings on the paper. You can choose among the following: short sayings, letters, prayers, parables, birth stories, passion stories, household codes, and sermons. Paste the pieces onto a new piece of computer or construction paper.

How the New Testament Grew

Divide a piece of licorice into three parts. Make the middle piece a tiny bit longer than the third piece. The first piece represents the time when Jesus lived and taught his followers how to live with concern for others. The second piece represents the time when people told stories about Jesus and Paul started to write his letters. The third piece represents the time of most of the writing, editing, and compiling of the New Testament. In summary, the three pieces represent the life of Jesus, oral tradition, and composition.

2

Looking at the New Testament Like an Artist

LINE, FORM, COLOR, AND texture are called the *formal art elements*. Artists and writers use them in different ways.

As you know, artists draw with lines. Sometimes the lines are straight. At other times the lines are curvy. Authors write with lines. The plot of a story is called the story line. In essays, the development of the main idea is sometimes referred to as a line of thought. When an author is not organizing material in a linear manner or a straight line, the writer "writes in circles."

Artists paint forms and sometimes start by looking at an object to see the most basic, underlying form. For example, the basic or underlying shape of a house is likely a rectangle. When writers talk about form, they mean the kind of literature, such as a poem, novel, short story, or even a form within a form, such as dialogue in a story. The form of writing that a writer chooses is the foundation on which he or she builds a story, or essay, or poem.

Artists paint colors, study colors, and discuss colors. Many people have a favorite color and feel nourished by colors. Writers refer to colors. Sometimes they have favorite words or phrases that color their writings.

Artists create texture from applying paint heavily or drawing lines that cross to suggest rough surfaces. Writers create texture by referring to other pieces of literature when, for example, a character in a story is reading. Texture also comes from tying together several plots in a story.

These formal art elements—line, form, color, and texture—are used by the biblical authors. In our exploration of the New Testament, we will look at these artistic characteristics. As in any kind of writing, line in the Bible can be a story line or a line of thought, whether the line is straight or curvy. Form is the kind of writing, the basic underlying form on which the author builds his or her work. Forms of writing in the New Testament, as we have seen, include sayings, stories, letters, prayers, poems, and lists.

Color as applied to biblical literature can include the author's favorite words that color the text. Color can also refer to an actual color, as, for example, the green grass in Mark's feeding of the five thousand people (Mark 6:30–42).

Texture in the New Testament is really fun to discover. Sometimes a passage in the New Testament refers to a passage in the Hebrew Scriptures. Drawing upon Old Testament passages gives richness, texture, and shades of meaning to New Testament writings. Texture shows continuity between the Old Testament and the New Testament. Continuity reminds us that Christianity is rooted in Judaism. One way to find texture is to look at the notes in a study bible such as *The HarperCollins Study Bible*.

Other artistic characteristics that I will use to describe biblical texts are focal point, perspective, contrast, and counterbalance. As we read the New Testament together, you will glimpse moments of artistry in the Bible. When you discover the New Testament authors' favorite words, their main ideas or focus, and their various understandings, you will see like an artist.

ACTIVITY

Paul Remembered the Hebrew Bible

To see an example of texture, read Rom 1:17 and Hab 2:4. The Letter to the Romans was written by Paul, who is sometimes called the *Apostle Paul* or *Saint Paul*. Do you think that Paul valued his spiritual ancestors in the Old Testament?

3

The Basic Story of Jesus's Life

THE BASIC HISTORICAL OUTLINE of Jesus's life is that he was born in Galilee early in the first century, grew up, taught, and healed people. He was crucified by the Roman government. The gospels of Matthew, Mark, and Luke are our main sources of information about Jesus.

Christians have added convictions that include belief in Jesus's resurrection and that his death was redeeming in some way. However, my concern in this chapter is to tell how the story of Jesus's life is recorded in the gospels of Matthew, Mark, and Luke.

Because Matthew, Mark, and Luke tell stories in almost the same way, their stories are called the Synoptic Gospels. The word *synoptic* is related to the words *sympathy* and *sync*. If you have a sympathetic friend, you and your friend would tell a story in sync, in a similar way. However, there are differences in Matthew's, Mark's, and Luke's stories, which are confusing and thus present a problem called the Synoptic Problem. Because of the Synoptic Problem, we must account for the differences in the stories.

The most common solution to the Synoptic Problem is that Mark was the first gospel to be written. Matthew and Luke followed Mark's outline of the life of Jesus and added information from a source of Jesus's sayings called *Q*, short for the German word *Quelle*, meaning "source." Then Matthew added his own sources called *M*, and Luke used his unique material called *L*. For example, Luke told long stories that Matthew and Mark do not tell, and therefore he had a story source and possibly made up stories to expand upon Jesus's message. Sometimes Luke corrects Mark's New Testament Greek. In summary, although Matthew, Mark, and Luke tell the story of Jesus in basically the same way, they paint different pictures of Jesus.

ACTIVITY

Changing a Story

You can do this exercise by yourself or in a group. However, a group project is helpful in seeing how different versions of a story happen. I will tell a snippet of a story, and you can change it to make it better or reflect your own knowledge.

> Sarah, age eight, and her mother, named Dorothy, planned a day at the beach. Sarah's mother asked Sarah to pack a large canvas bag with snacks, toys for herself, and toys for her cousin Peter, age five. They planned to meet Peter and his mother at the beach. Sarah packed three chocolate bars, four apples, and five oranges. She added a Barbie doll, a box of Barbie accessories, three small trucks, and a sand pail.

Pretend that you know Sarah, her mother, Peter, and his mother. Change the story if you feel that you can add important details or corrections. You may know something about these people that I do not know. For example, you may know what snacks or toys Sarah likes best. Did Sarah forget anything? You may have a source of information about electronic toys that I do not have. Your *special toy source* is something like Matthew's or Luke's special sources. My math may look suspicious, and you may wish to correct it. If you want to, you can finish the story. Then you would be a writer like Luke who told longer stories to explain the teachings of Jesus.

After you are done, your class can compare stories. How do you account for the different stories?

PART 1

The Story of Jesus and How It Spread

4

The Gospel according to Mark

Because Matthew is the first book in the New Testament, you must wonder why we are starting with Mark's gospel. You may have guessed. Mark was the first New Testament author to write a gospel, which seems to be a form that he invented.[1] He wrote in about AD 70, likely in Rome.

Mark may have been an interpreter of Peter, who was an eyewitness to Jesus. Mark heard stories about Jesus and probably read some others. He spoke Greek but struggled to write it well. Speaking poetically, Mark wore dark sunglasses and focused on the meaning of the cross and suffering. Mark's core belief (10:45) is that Jesus came to serve and give his life as a ransom for many. These reasons for Jesus's life and sacrificial death are recorded between two stories of restored sight in 8:22–26 and in 10:46–52. Mark's summary can be compared to a sandwich filling in between two pieces of bread, which represent the two stories of restored sight. This sandwich-like arrangement shows how important it was to Mark that people see and comprehend his understanding of Jesus.

---

1. Harrington, *Who Is Jesus?* 21.

As we have seen, Mark wrote a gospel. His gospel was something like biographies in the ancient world about leaders who were willing to die for their people. However, Mark's gospel is a theological story about Jesus the Christ. In time, the word *gospel* came to mean not only a form of writing but also the gospel proclamation about God's love shown in Jesus's living and loving.

ARTISTIC FEATURES

The artistic elements that most help us understand Mark are color and line. Mark's favorite words that color his writing are *no faith*, *immediately*, and *amazed*. To Mark, the disciples had *no faith*, and people were *amazed* at Jesus's power to heal. The word *immediately* adds to the fast pace of Mark's gospel. Mark is the only gospel writer to tell us that the grass is green in stories of miraculous feedings. The hint is that like the good shepherd of Ps 23, Jesus is the good shepherd for the people who are like sheep without a shepherd in Mark 6:34.

Mark's plot line is that Jesus, in keeping with God's plan, had to suffer. This plot line is broken into two parts. In chapters 1–8, Jesus proclaims God's kingdom by teaching and healing in Galilee. The kingdom of God is a time of worship, peace, justice, and good will among people. People in the kingdom will follow Jesus's ethical teachings and give shelter to one another. In chapters 9–16, Jesus takes his disciples on an educational trip between Galilee and Jerusalem and predicts his suffering and death. The ending of Mark is like a two-pronged fork. The longer collage-like ending is in 16:9–19 and includes post-resurrection experiences that were most likely added to Mark by editors who pasted together stories from the other gospels. Because Mark was the first person to write the outline of Jesus's life, I will give a short chapter-by-chapter summary.

PART 1: PROCLAIMING GOD'S KINGDOM BY TEACHING AND HEALING

Chapter 1

Jesus is baptized by John and tempted in the wilderness where he dwells peacefully with wild animals.

Chapter 2

Jesus tells a paralyzed man that his sins are forgiven before telling him to take up his bed and walk.

Chapter 3

Jesus says that the Sabbath was made for people and heals a man with a withered hand.

Chapter 4

Jesus tells parables about the kingdom of God, which will grow from small to large.

Chapter 5

Jesus heals a woman and a twelve-year-old girl.

Chapter 6

Jesus is rejected in his hometown but feeds five thousand people with five fish and two loaves of bread.

Chapter 7

Jesus broadens his ministry to include non-Jews by healing a Syrophoenician woman's daughter.

Chapter 8

Mark tells another story of feeding the multitudes with slightly different details. Maybe there were two feedings or perhaps Mark heard two stories and wanted to include both in his gospel. Jesus heals a blind man and teaches his disciples about his identity and about the cost of discipleship.

PART 2: JESUS TAKES THE DISCIPLES ON AN EDUCATIONAL TRIP

Chapter 9

The transfiguration symbolizes Jesus's participation in God's glory.

Chapter 10

Jesus stresses the hazards of wealth and tells of his death for the third time.

Chapter 11

Jesus enters Jerusalem on the day Christians call Palm Sunday.

Chapter 12

In answering questions about taxes, Jesus says to give to the emperor the things that belong to the emperor and to give to God the things that are God's.

Chapter 13

No one knows for sure what this chapter means. My best thought is that people in Jesus's movement or the budding church who are worried about the future or maybe the actual loss of the temple can expect ongoing persecution and future vindication.

Chapter 14

Jesus and his disciples gather for a Passover meal and Jesus tells the disciples that one of them will betray him.

Chapter 15

Jesus is handed over to be crucified.

Chapter 16

Three women visit the tomb, and a young man tells them that Jesus has been raised. You noticed that I used the passive tense in the words "has been raised." Sometimes the passive tense is called the "theological passive" because the New Testament Greek form of the verb suggests that God raised Jesus. He did not just get up by himself like getting up from a chair. We do not know how exactly God raised Jesus. Beliefs range from insisting on a physical resurrection to trusting in an ever-increasing understanding of Jesus's teachings. A middle ground is considering the resurrection of Jesus as like unto Paul's description of sowing in a physical body and rising in a spiritual body (1 Cor 15:44).

ACTIVITY

From Seed to Shelter

Read Mark 4:30–32. Paste a real seed or draw one on the bottom of a piece of paper. Then draw a large shrub, or take artistic license and draw a tree. Add birds. They can be realistic or imaginative. Your picture will remind you that Mark pictured the kingdom of God as growing from small to large and as becoming a place of shelter.

5

The Gospel according to Matthew

MATTHEW WAS AN ANONYMOUS, Greek-speaking author named after the Matthew who had been Jesus's disciple. A verse in his gospel (13:52) paints a cameo picture of him as a scribe in training who draws out of his treasure what is new and what is old. Thus Matthew valued his Jewish roots and found new treasures in the teaching of Jesus.

Matthew was attracted to Jesus, the wise teacher who taught in parables. Therefore Matthew recorded and organized Jesus's teachings. He wrote between AD 85 and 90 when the church started to take shape. His gospel is a document for the new community of Jews and Gentiles joined together in the spirit of Christ.

Matthew draws a picture of a wise and loving God who established Sabbath rest at the beginning of creation. He bases his story on Mark and has his own special sources, *M*. Matthew was motivated by a religious crisis that faced all Jews in the first century.[1] The temple had been destroyed. Judaism was in transition. How could Judaism continue without the temple? Matthew explains Jesus as the promise

---

1. Harrington, *Who Is Jesus?* 29.

to Israel and fulfillment of the Hebrew law, a kind of updated Moses. Matthew's Jesus offers both challenge and comfort. There is comfort in the beatitudes (5:3–11) and challenge in the call to forgive (18:21–22). Peter is important in Matthew both for his faith in Jesus as the Messiah and as a founding figure of the church.

ARTISTIC FEATURES

Line

Segmented Line

Matthew understands history as a segmented line. The first line is a list of Jesus's ancestors. The second segment is Jesus's time on earth. The third part is the fulfillment of the kingdom.

Forms

Building Blocks

Matthew organizes Jesus's message into five sermons. The most important one is called the *Sermon on the Mount* (Matt 5–7). The other sermons include the missionary discourse (10), community discourse (18), and eschatological discourse, or discussion of the future (24–25).

Bookends

Sayings that promise that God is Emmanuel, meaning "God is with us," are like bookends at the beginning and end of Matthew (1:22–23 and 28:19–20). Please pause here, look up these passages, and read them.

List of Ancestors

Matthew begins with a list of Jesus's ancestors. When I was in college, my professor stressed that the inclusions of Ruth, who was from Moab, and Rahab, who was a Gentile, suggest universality. Thirty years later in graduate school, my professor noted that the inclusion of women in the list suggests inclusiveness. The combined hint is that the kingdom will be inclusive.

Birth Story

Matthew's birth story includes the wise men, which foreshadow the wise grown-up Jesus.

Parables

The kingdom of God is in the center of Matthew's gospel and is his central concern. As a central concern, it is a focal point. The definition of a parable, almost always quoted from C. H. Dodd, is "a metaphor or simile drawn from nature or common life, arresting the hearer by its vividness or strangeness, and leaving the mind in sufficient doubt about its precise application to tease it into active thought."[2] The first parable (13:1–8) is about seeds that fall on a path, seeds that fall on rocky ground, and seeds that fall on good soil. The seeds that fall on good soil grow like disciples who bear fruit. Another parable compares the growing kingdom to a woman who mixes yeast into flour to make bread rise (13:33).

Passion Story

The story of Jesus's passion is told in Matthew 27.

---

2. Duling and Perrin, *New Testament*, 603.

Color Words

Little Faith

Mark described the disciples as having no faith. Matthew upgrades them to little faith (6:30, 8:26, 14:31, 16:8).

New Testament stories about Jesus addressing controversial issues of his day with his opponents are called *controversy stories*. In a controversy story about conflicting views, Jesus speaks to the scribes and Pharisees, who were religious leaders, and distills the weightier matter of the law as "justice, mercy, and faith" (23:23).

Fulfill

Fulfill is a favorite word of Matthew's that suggests that Jesus fulfills the law and prophets. For example, see 4:14.

Fruit

Matthew uses the word *fruit* to connote good living. In 12:33 Jesus says that the tree is known by its fruit. One implication is that people are also known by their fruit or by ways of living that nourish other people. In Matt 25, Jesus complains about people not giving food to the hungry and drink to the thirsty, nor visiting the sick and those in prison. He concludes with the words, "'Truly I tell you, just as you did not do it to the least of these, you did not do it to me'" (25:45). (This verse, which is very important in Matthew's understanding, is from Matthew's special *M* source.) People with a wide variety of beliefs who do feed the hungry and visit the sick are bearing most excellent fruit.

Perfect

The word *perfect* scares people. In Matthew's thought, it does not mean perfectionism. It means wholeness. Life is more whole when people mature in thought and grow in caring.

ACTIVITY

Reading the Greatest Sermon Ever Spoken

Please read the Sermon on the Mount in chapters 5–7.

6

The Gospel according to Luke

THE WRITER OF THE Gospel of Luke, whom we will call Luke in deference to tradition, was an anonymous writer and editor. Because he was literary and thoughtful, he was suited to his self-assigned task of writing an orderly account so that his patron, Theophilus, would know the truth about the things he had been taught (1:1–4). In Greek, *Theophilus* means "lover of God." Luke was an educated Greek man who wrote for Gentiles. Before becoming a follower of Jesus, he may have been a "God-fearer." People known as "God-fearers" were attracted to Judaism because it emphasized ethical conduct and belief in one God. Belief in one God who wants people to be ethical is called *ethical monotheism*.

Luke wore rose-colored glasses. While in Mark's thought, taking up the cross would likely mean martyrdom, Luke had a broader, more integrated, day-to-day concept of sacrificial living (2:1–20). A person who follows Luke's vision of sacrificial living will pay attention to God each day and will honor concepts such as beauty, truth, and justice. By doing these things, people will be lifted up beyond themselves.

Luke wrote his gospel between AD 85 and 90. He also wrote Acts and therefore authored a two-volume set. Southern Greece may have been the place of composition.

Luke pictures Jesus as God's Son, the centerpiece of history, the glory of Israel, and the light to the Gentiles. In Luke's understanding, the prophets of the past are in the spiritual history of Israel. Jesus is the centerpiece of history. The work of the Holy Spirit continues into the future. To Luke, Jesus is God's Son from the beginning. Jesus's identity is proclaimed by the angels in the birth story (2:10). When Jesus was about twelve years old, he told his parents that he must be in his Father's house (2:49); thus he was aware of his relationship with God his Father and his special role in the history of Israel.

ARTISTIC FEATURES

Themes

Luke develops themes in his gospel, so a good way to study Luke is to consider his themes.

Joy

Joy is woven through this gospel and ties the story together. When John's mother Elizabeth hears Mary's greetings, John, who is still in Elizabeth's womb, jumps for joy (1:41). When Jesus is born, an angel tells shepherds not to be afraid because he brings good news of great joy for all the people (2:10). When the risen Jesus appears to the disciples, they are "in their joy" (24:41). After Jesus's resurrection, the disciples return to Jerusalem with great joy and continue to bless God in the temple (24:52–53).

Reversals

In chapter 1, Mary's song foreshadows Jesus's concern for the poor. She sings about reversals or turnarounds: "He has brought down the powerful from their thrones, and lifted up the lowly; he has filled the hungry with good things, and sent the rich away empty" (1:52–53). In Nazareth, when the grown-up Jesus speaks, he reads from the prophet Isaiah: "The Spirit of the Lord is upon me, because he has anointed me to bring good news to the poor" (4:18).

Dangers of Wealth

Luke's concern about wealth is that money can be idolized or become our ultimate concern. The parable of the rich man and Lazarus in 16:19–31 combines the themes of reversals and idolizing of money. (The Lazarus in this story is not the same Lazarus as the Lazarus who was raised from the dead.)

Concern for the Lost and Lonely

Luke paints a picture of Jesus as concerned for the lost and lonely and for the outcasts and ostracized. In Luke 15, three stories show Jesus's concern for the lost. These stories are the parable of the lost sheep (vv. 1–7), the parable of the lost coin (vv. 8–10), and the parable of the prodigal son (vv. 11–32).

Compassion

Nonjudgmental compassion is Jesus's standard of justice in Luke's account. He wants his disciples to share in his compassion and teaches that the measure of compassion we show will be the measure we receive (6:38). The father's forgiveness of his prodigal son, which symbolizes God's forgiveness, is the deepest compassion a human can express.

Prayer

In Luke, Jesus prays at decisive points. He prays before choosing the twelve disciples (6:12). On the Mount of Olives, Jesus prays that if it is God's will, his cup of suffering will be removed (22:42). His greatest prayer is for God's forgiveness of the people who crucify him. "Father, forgive them for they do not know what they are doing" (23:34).

Heavenly Banquet

Luke is convinced that all will be welcome in the kingdom of God. He explains that welcome in the parable of the great dinner (14:15–24).

Word and Sacrament

In a post-resurrection experience, the disciples have burning hearts when Jesus opens the Scriptures to them and they recognize him in the breaking of the bread. Scripture is a symbol of word. Bread suggests sacrament. You can read the whole story about the walk to Emmaus in 24:13–35.

Holy Spirit

The Holy Spirit is present at Jesus's baptism (3:21–22) and helps Jesus withstand temptation in the wilderness (4:1–13). Luke will continue to write about the Holy Spirit in the Acts of the Apostles.

ACTIVITIES

Looking at Art

Georges Rouault's painting *Christ in the Outskirts* shows Christ with two small children on the outskirts of a town. Rouault's picture of Christ matches Luke's verbal picture of Jesus who is concerned for miserable and marginal people. You can find the picture in *Sister Wendy's 1000 Masterpieces: Sister Wendy Beckett's Selection of the Greatest Paintings in Western Art*.[1]

Reading and Thinking about Other People

Luke paints a picture of Jesus as concerned for the lost and lonely and for the outcasts and ostracized. In his story of the good Samaritan, the Samaritan, who is an outcast, is the only person to help a man who had been left for dead at the side of the road (Luke 10:25–37). Left for dead is another form of being an outcast. The Samaritan, who was a good neighbor, knew how important it is to help people in need. One outcast knew how to help another outcast.

Read the story. Do you identify with either the good Samaritan or the man by the side of the road? Has anyone ever been a good Samaritan to you? Sometimes we learn about being a good Samaritan when a good Samaritan comes to our aid, as did a gas station attendant who helped my family on an Easter Sunday afternoon in 1978 when our car broke down just off the George Washington Bridge in New York City. Even his German shepherd guard dog was friendly and let our daughter Amy, at the time age six, pet him. Have you

---

1. Beckett, *Sister Wendy's 1000 Masterpieces*, 401.

had an experience that helps you to be sensitive to the needs of others? How can you help someone, known or unknown to you, who is lonely, hungry, or hurting?

7

The Acts of the Apostles

Luke and Acts are a two-volume set by a Gentile Christian. Both are dedicated to Theophilus. In Acts, Luke wrote salvation history because he believed that God's purposes are working out in history. (*Salvation history* is historical reporting that includes how the author believes God is working to bring faith and trust, health and wholeness to people.) Even though he was not concerned with details of events, he places his stories and sermons in history. If you wish, relax and read the story as faithful, historical fiction. Acts is an adventure story with theological meaning. It was written around AD 85–90 outside of Palestine. Luke wanted to show how early Christianity spread from Jerusalem to Rome. Luke's perspective is that by the power of the Holy Spirit, the gospel message will spread throughout the world. The use of the editorial "we" suggests that Luke might have been a traveling companion of Paul.

As more people join along the way, requirements of faith are simplified. Understanding of God's grace grows. People known as "God-fearers," who were attracted to Jewish belief in one God but found food laws and circumcision off-putting joined the early Christian movement that was becoming more inclusive. Let us take a fast-paced survey with postcard jottings from Paul's journey. Contemporary readers will find two main parts: (1) the church starts, and (2) the church spreads.

THE CHURCH STARTS

Chapter 1

After the resurrection but before ascension, Jesus appears to his disciples.

By casting lots, the apostles choose Matthias to replace Judas (vv. 24–26).

Chapter 2

Compressing the time that it took for the Christian movement to develop from Judaism, Luke tells the story of the church's birthday, when people spoke in different languages but understood one another.

Chapter 3

Faith and trust start to open up for Gentiles as well as Jews.

Chapter 4

Peter and John are arrested but are released.

Chapter 5

Ananias and his wife, Sapphira do not share as they had promised. Therefore, they are struck down and die. Thinking about the implications of the story for today, I ponder how greed and failure to share cause people to self-destruct.

Gamaliel, a teacher of the law, suggests leaving the Christian movement alone because developing Christian witness, worship, and work might be inspired by God.

Chapter 6

Church administrators are picked to run the church's meals program.

Chapter 7

Stephen concludes that God is bigger than the temple or human institutions (7:48–50). His insight is not well received and he is stoned. Like Jesus on the cross, he asked that the sins of his killers not be held against them (vv. 58–60).

Chapter 8

Saul persecutes the church. Phillip explains to a man from Ethiopia that Jesus is like the sheep led to slaughter in the Old Testament book of Isaiah.

Chapter 9

Saul, later called Paul, has a life-altering experience, or conversion, on the road to Damascus and changes his mind about the new religious movement. He is blinded by a great light and hears Jesus asking him why he persecutes him. Paul comes to believe that he has been chosen to bring Jesus and his way to the Gentiles. Peter heals Tabitha. The news gets around.

Chapter 10

Peter realizes that anyone who does what is right is acceptable to God and that the Holy Spirit has been poured out to the Gentiles.

Chapter 11

Barnabas and Saul go to Antioch where the disciples are first called Christians (v. 26).

Chapter 12

Peter is imprisoned, but an angel frees him.

THE CHURCH SPREADS

Chapter 13

Paul shares his belief that God wants him to be a light for the Gentiles (v. 47).

Chapter 14

Paul reflects on signs from nature of God's goodness.

Chapter 15

Personal experiences of inclusive fellowship are distilled and translated into church life and rules.

Chapter 16

Lydia, who already worshiped God, joins the movement. Paul and Silas upset a man with a fortune-telling business and go to jail. They are freed by an earthquake. The jailer becomes a believer (vv. 25–34).

Chapter 17

Paul tells the people of Athens that they should not worship idols. Paul poetically says that in God "we live and move and have our being" (v. 28).

Chapter 18

Paul goes to Corinth and then to Ephesus.

Chapter 19

In Ephesus, Paul criticizes the making of silver idols. A wise town clerk tells people to cool down because Paul did not break the law.

Chapter 20

Paul sets out for Greece.

Chapter 21

Paul and crew sail on to Rhodes and eventually to Jerusalem. Paul is arrested, but the tribune who arrested him realizes that Paul is not the Egyptian who stirred up a revolt (v. 38). Paul asks to speak to the people.

Chapter 22

Paul speaks in Hebrew (v. 2) and says that God has sent him to the Gentiles.

Chapter 23

Paul's nephew overcomes a plot against Paul, and the tribune (vv. 16–22) protects Paul. Paul is sent to Felix, governor in Caesarea.

Chapter 24

Felix leaves Paul in prison.

Chapter 25

Festus, who succeeds Felix, tells Paul that because he appealed to the emperor he will go to the emperor.

Chapter 26

Paul tells the story of his experience on the road to Damascus and restates the importance of proclamation to the Gentiles. If Paul had not appealed to the emperor, he could have been freed (v. 32).

Chapter 27

Paul is sent on a boat to Italy with other prisoners. A northeast storm blows up. An angel tells Paul that because he has to stand before the governor all on board will be safe. The prisoners eat together in a way that echoes the Last Supper and foreshadows the Eucharist. The boat strikes a reef. All swim safely to shore.

Chapter 28

Paul and the prisoners land on Malta. Paul heals people who are so thankful that when it is time to sail again they stock the ship with provisions. In Rome, Paul is held in a kind of house arrest but continues his preaching ministry. The story is open ended because we do not know for certain if Paul dies in prison or is martyred.

ACTIVITY

Telling Your Own Story

Your story of your spiritual journey has just begun. You may want to think about your faith and how it is growing. Have there been ups and downs, sad or happy times? If you wish, share your thoughts in discussion or by writing.

PART 2

John and His Community
of Loving Friends

8

The Gospel according to John

GOD SO LOVED THE WORLD

Most likely, the primary author of the Gospel of John was a Jewish Christian who was a student of the beloved disciple. Featured in John's gospel, the beloved disciple is an anonymous person who became a model follower. This disciple passed on traditions to the primary author. After the primary author did his work, an editor added material. For example, the image of Jesus as the bread of life in John 6:35 may have been rounded out in 6:51–58 by the editor, who may have wanted to emphasize the importance of the Eucharist.

John wrote a poetic and theological gospel. His gospel is very different from the gospels of Matthew, Mark, and Luke. John was written around AD 90, but the author might have had some pre-Markan sources of passion and resurrection stories. John may have been written in Ephesus. Others say Syria.

One of the author's reasons for writing is so people may come to believe that Jesus is the Messiah and have life in his name (20:30–31). Despite the words, "come to believe," this gospel was not intended to be a missionary tract, according to Fr. Daniel J. Harrington, SJ, in his book *Who Is Jesus? Why Is He Important?* Most likely, the gospel was written to help believers adjust to life outside of the synagogue.[1]

Imagine the predicament of the Jews who had been expelled from the synagogue for following Jesus. These people who were asked to leave may even have been included in a prayer against heretics, a benediction from the rabbinical tradition between AD 80 and 90. The expelled Jews had been faithful in worship and practice all their lives. Yet they had been a bit different for years. Perhaps middle-aged parents told their young adult children that their great-grandfathers and -grandmothers said that there was no earthly reason for Jesus to be put to death. The Romans did not have a strong legal case. Jesus was a good Jew who opened up an understanding of righteous living and the love of God to Jews and non-Jewish people.

The Jews who were interested in the teachings of Jesus could not go back to their synagogue. They had beliefs that set them apart. They believed that Jesus was superior to Moses and found wisdom in Jesus. Their central confession that forced separation was that Jesus is Messiah (9:22). Coming to grips with how you understand Jesus is part of John's theology.

The persecuted community was like the blind man whose spiritual sight increased as his faith in Jesus grew (9:1–41). Thus, the story of the blind man is about an individual and also about the conflict when the Jews who broke away grew in faith. There was no turning back. Even hope for a rebuilt temple lost appeal. The developing Christian

---

1. Harrington, *Who Is Jesus?* 61.

movement was the best choice for Jewish Christians in the ancient world. The only possible way for members of John's community to connect with God was through Jesus; belief in God as Word and Wisdom was clarified in Jesus. People in the Johannine community experienced new life and found nourishment in Jesus, who was for them the bread of life. Throughout the gospel, John's emphasis is on joy made complete, and on the earthly foretaste of eternal life through believing (5:24).

Followers then and now find joy in John 3:16, which well may be the most beloved passage in the New Testament: "For God so loved the world that he gave his only Son, so that everyone who believes in him may not perish but may have eternal life." Most often this verse is understood to mean that believers will have eternal life in the hereafter. Another interpretation is that people who believe in Jesus's ethic of service, compassion, and forgiveness will be part of an ongoing movement that will matter forever.

DISTINCTIVE FEATURES

Way of Talking

In this gospel, Jesus does not speak in parables and rarely mentions the kingdom of God. Jesus speaks in both long discourses and short, iconic statements. Chapter 10, about Jesus the good shepherd, provides an example of a long explanation and short pithy statement. Verses 1–21 are the long story of Jesus as the good shepherd. The short, iconic statement is, "I am the good shepherd" (10:11). People do not talk in normal conversation like Jesus does in John. So the style of Jesus's speech is a big hint that this gospel is a *theological* writing.

High Contrasts in Black and White

Throughout the gospel there is high contrast between light and darkness.

Belief That Jesus Is Preexistent

In John, Jesus believes that he was preexistent with God.

Meaning of Jesus's Birth

Matthew and Luke tell birth stories. John does not have a birth story but draws out the meaning of Jesus's birth in a beautiful sentence: "The light shines in the darkness, and the darkness did not overcome it" (1:5).

Anger Foreshadowing the Future

The cleansing of the temple occurs at the start of Jesus's ministry rather than towards the end as in the Synoptic Gospels. Jesus is angrier in John's account, and this anger foreshadows the end of his life.

Time of the Last Supper

In the Synoptic Gospels, the Last Supper was a Passover meal. In John it is a pre-Passover meal. A pre-Passover meal suggests that the crucifixion of Jesus on Passover means that Jesus was the sacrificial lamb.

Textured Picture of the Holy Spirit

In John, the Holy Spirit or Counselor has several roles. The Counselor is like a friend who will keep people from being lonely (14:15–16). The Counselor is also a teacher who will remind people of what Jesus said (14:26). As witness, the Counselor will testify about Jesus in the Spirit of Truth (16:7–11).

Counterbalance

The Gospel of John often states in one way or another that Jesus is the only way to God. However, even though the gospel was authored at a time when Christian Jews broke away from the conservative synagogue and had to make a strong case for their way to God, there are hints of God's universal acceptance. "The true light, which enlightens everyone, was coming into the world" (1:9). If you wish, see also 3:19 and 5:28–29 where a person's good deeds count toward eternal life.

Jesus as Logos

In John, Jesus is the Logos. Shades of meaning in the word *logos* include, "word and language of God," "wisdom and thought," "light and truth." The word *logic* is related to logos. The prologue in John, which is a poetic hymn, introduces Jesus as the incarnate Word in the first five verses of John's gospel. (The word *incarnate* means "in the flesh.") This lovely poem of light and love follows.

> In the beginning was the Word, and the Word was with God, and the Word was God. He was in the beginning with God.

All things came into being through him, and without him not one thing came into being. What has come into being in him was life, and the life was the light of all people. The light shines in the darkness, and the darkness did not overcome it" (1:1–5)

THE TWO-PART LINE OF THE TEXT

Following the prologue, John is divided into two parts. In the first part, called the "Book of Signs," Jesus draws many kinds of people to him. Miracles are signs of his grace and power. Titles define him. In the second part, which is called the "Book of Glory," Jesus instructs his disciples and glorifies God by finishing his earthly work.

Part 1: The Book of Signs

Jesus is revealed through actions and titles in the "Book of Signs." In chapter 2, Jesus changes water into wine at a wedding. Another sign of Jesus's power is told in a story in which Jesus heals an officer's son (4:46–54).

The image of bread, prominent in chapter 6, must have been especially appealing to Samaritans, who like Moses, worshipped in a mountain wilderness where nourishment was scarce. The author of John reminds his readers that God gave their ancestors manna or bread from heaven during their days in the wilderness (6:31). Jesus is revealed as the new Moses, the Bread of Life, which sustains like Old Testament manna in the wilderness: "I am the bread of life. Whoever comes to me will never be hungry, and whoever believes in me will never be thirsty" (v. 35).

Whether the voice of the early church or a belief in the heart of Jesus, Jesus is recorded as uttering an iconic statement: "I am the light of the world" (8:12). For the people of John's community, truth shown like a light in Jesus. Changes in perspective were liberating for them: "Then Jesus said to the Jews who had believed in him, 'If you continue in my word, you are truly my disciples; and you will know the truth, and the truth will make you free'" (8:31–32).

Part 2: The Book of Glory

The "Book of Glory" is John chapters 13–20. (Chapter 21 may be a later addition.) In this book, as the title implies, Jesus glorifies God by finishing his early work.

In preparing for his death, Jesus washes the feet of his disciples, foretells his betrayal (13:2–5), and gives the new commandment that we love one another as he loves us. He adds that people will know that we are disciples by our love for one another (vv. 34–35).

Chapters 14–16 are Jesus's farewell address. The highlight of chapter 14 is Jesus's promise not to leave his followers orphaned. He tells us that we should not be afraid nor let our hearts be troubled. Jesus promises to send the Holy Spirit or Advocate.

In chapter 17, Jesus prays for his disciples in a prayer that is a kind of earthly ascension. He glorifies God by finishing his earthly work. He lived to the glory of God and would soon die to the glory of God.

In chapter 18, Jesus is arrested. Peter denies Jesus. Jesus appears before Pilate and tells him that his kingdom is not of this world. Chapter 19 is the heart of the passion story, or story of Jesus's death, and movingly tells of Jesus giving up his spirit to God. In chapter 20, Mary Magdalene discovers the empty tomb. Jesus appears to her, and at first she thinks he is the gardener but then recognizes him as her Teacher. Jesus also appears to the disciples and even convinces Thomas of his presence.

Chapter 21 may be a later addition, but it is a great one. Being fishermen, the disciples went right back to work after the resurrection. Like fishermen anywhere, they stop for breakfast, and the risen Jesus joins them. He asks Peter three times if Peter loves him. Three times Peter says "yes." Over the years, I have heard sermons that suggest that because Peter denied Jesus three times, his three fold declaration of love means that Jesus and Peter were reconciled. Jesus, the good shepherd, tells Peter to feed his lambs (21:15). Peter is called to be a shepherd like Jesus. Good shepherds make good pastors, and good pastors make good churches. The rest of the story of John's continuing community is told in the Letters of John.

ACTIVITY

Drawing Pictures of Jesus's Iconic Statements

If you are in a class, and you do not like to draw ask one person to draw, and photocopy the drawing for you to color and add your own touches.

I Am Sayings in the Gospel of John

Here are I Am Sayings that are verbal icons of Jesus, like picture icons on a computer screen.

6:35	Bread of life
6:51	Living bread
8:12	Light of the world
10:7–9	Gate for the sheep

10:11–14	Good shepherd
15:1–5	True vine

I Am Sayings That Use Abstract Nouns to Explain Who Jesus Is to John's Community

(These I am sayings are not as pictorial, but you might like to have them for future reference.)

11:25–6	Resurrection and the life
14:6	Way, truth, life

Summary of I Am Sayings That Imply That Jesus, Like God, Is the Great I Am

Moses first experienced God as I am (Exod 3:14). Because John describes Jesus in I am images, the suggestion is that Jesus is God. Another interpretation is that Jesus is a great and unique individual. The word *I* can connote a unique individual. The word *am* hints at largeness of being. Capital letters underscore greatness as humanity's best. Whether you believe that Jesus is God or the greatest human being or both, affirmation of his life and teachings empowers his followers, including you, to take courage and to take joy.

4:26	I am the one speaking.
6:20	I am, do not be afraid.
8:24	Believe that I am.
8:28	You will realize that I am.
8:58	Before Abraham was, I am.
13:19	You may come to believe that I am.
18:5–7	I am.

9

The Letters of First, Second, and Third John

FIRST JOHN: ABIDING IN LOVE AND GOD

First John is an encouraging, poetic essay that was most likely written in Ephesus around AD 100. Martin Luther said that it could buoy up afflicted hearts.[1] John Wesley found it to be a deep summary of genuine Christianity.[2] The author was not the same John who wrote the Gospel of John, but we will call him John. He wanted faithful people to carry on traditional beliefs and practices. His early Christian listeners needed to remember that Jesus was a historical person. If his people denied the full humanity of Jesus, they robbed themselves of the consolations from knowing that Jesus understands what it means to be human. John wanted his people to believe that they have eternal life (5:13). In contrast to the Gospel of John, in which Jesus is the incarnate Word, in 1 John the term "word of life" is a proclamation about Jesus. In 1 John, sinners or people who mess up have an advocate in Jesus (2:1–2). A common belief is that when

1. *New Interpreter's Bible*, 12:378.
2. Ibid, 365.

we pray, Jesus as advocate may make our situations clear to God, the Father. People who do not believe in God might find that if they followed Jesus's ethics, their good living will serve as advocate.

The most striking artistic feature of 1 John is curvy line. The author writes in a circular manner and returns to different ways of saying that God is love. "Beloved, let us love one another, because love is from God; everyone who loves is born of God and knows God" (4:7). "God is love, and those who abide in love abide in God, and God abides in them" (4:16).

SECOND JOHN: LOVE ONE ANOTHER

Second John is a letter with a black-and-white approach to conflict. This letter, also written around AD 100, probably in Ephesus, continues the theme of loving one another. This letter, written by an anonymous elder, was written to the "elect lady" who might be an individual or a symbol for the community. He warns the congregation about people who do not believe that Jesus was a real man who lived on earth. The advice to love one another, but to not be too nice to outsiders (1:10–11) was a form of protection.

THIRD JOHN: GREET FRIENDS AND IMITATE WHAT IS GOOD

Third John was written around AD 100 in Ephesus probably by the same person who wrote 2 John. It is a picture of a divided church and letter of recommendation for Gaius who practiced hospitality to missionaries. This hospitality empowered people to be coworkers with the truth. The author is afraid of doctrinal contamination. Perhaps the most significant passage is, "Beloved, do not imitate what is evil but imitate what is good. Whoever does good is from God; whoever does evil has not seen God" (v. 11).

ACTIVITIES

Thinking about God's Geometry

A derivative concept that I call God's geometry has stood up over time. The only math I really loved was geometry, which I learned in my sophomore year of high school in 1959–60. I wondered, as have other young people over the years, if the existence of God could be proven through geometric reasoning. No, apparently not. However, at church camp the next summer, our teachers, who were Congregational ministers and seminary students, gave us campers a diagram in the form of a triangle. God was named at one point, other people at another point, and oneself at the remaining point on the triangle. The idea is that the three-pointed triangle is a symbol of relationships and the flow of love. So even if geometry could not prove that God exists, a geometric shape could describe a right relationship to God, one another, and to ourselves as individuals. In college I brought up this concept to the delight of my Methodist professors. This diagram has staying power. There is a more detailed version called the "Circuit of Love" in 1 John in the *New Interpreter's Bible*.[3] It is my hope that even when the details about the Letters of John, or the nature of the church disputes in John's community fade in importance, you will still recall God's love triangle. Unlike human love triangles that generally de-

---

3. *New Interpreter's Bible*, 12:436.

scribe a competitive, romantic relationship, God's geometry keeps divine love in circulation.

Embroidery or Computer Graphics

When I was in the third grade, the girls in our church group embroidered the words God is love in cross-stitch. The fabric was natural muslin and about eight by eight inches square. We used red embroidery floss with two strands. The adult leaders did the cross-stitch design in pencil and made a fringe on the outside edge of the square. Today there are indelible markers and fabric paint that could be used instead of pencil. You could do a transfer pattern on a computer. Over thirty years later, when helping fourth grade girls do this same project, I found that they liked to do this project in split stitch as well as cross-stitch. You could draw the words God is love and stitch the words with split stitch. To do this stitch, simply make one stitch any size you want. Come up through the middle of the stitch and make another. Keep going.

If you do not want to embroider, you could just use fabric paint. Also, instead of embroidery, you could design a page with the words God is love on your computer. There are so many fonts that the selection of type is an art in itself. Your teachers may have other ideas.

PART 3

Paul and His Writing Friends

10

Introducing Paul

YOU HAVE ALREADY BRIEFLY met Paul in the chapter on the Acts of the Apostles. That book provides supplemental details about Paul's life, but the main sources of information about Paul come from the letters he wrote.

Probably, Paul was born in Taurus between AD 5 and 10 and was educated there. He studied with Gamaliel, who was a famous rabbi. Paul wrote in Greek and quoted from the Greek version of the Hebrew Scriptures. He studied speech writing and also learned tent making, which came in handy later on as a way of supporting himself so he would not be a burden to the faith communities. Tarsus was a city where Paul could learn about Gentiles, pagans, and philosophers. Paul was a Roman citizen. Saul was his Jewish name, and Paul was his name as a Roman citizen and also the name he was known by after a life-changing experience.

Saul persecuted the church with zeal (Acts 8:1–3; Gal 1:13–17). Then he had a life-changing experience. On the road to Damascus, Paul experienced a blinding light and heard a voice saying, "Saul, Saul, why do you persecute me?" (Acts 9:4). He understood the voice as the call of Jesus. However his encounter occurred, for Paul, this experience meant that the crucifixion and the scandal of the cross were not the end of Jesus's story. The story of the risen Christ continued.

Motivated by his conviction of the abiding love of God, Paul felt called to preach and establish assemblies or new churches. He wrote at least seven letters and inspired the next generation of letter writers who wrote in Paul's line of thought. The letters that Paul definitely wrote are 1 Thessalonians, 1 Corinthians, 2 Corinthians, Philippians, Philemon, Galatians, and Romans.

Paul was not as interested in the wise sayings of Jesus and the kingdom of God as he was in the understanding of the risen Christ as a reconciler who welcomes all into the family of God. In this family, "There is no longer Jew or Greek, there is no longer slave or free, there is no longer male and female; for all of you are one in Christ Jesus" (Gal 3:28).

ACTIVITY

Creating a Card of Grace and Peace

Paul's letters are both similar and different from letters in his culture. Paul follows the basic form that includes an introduction, central section, and conclusion. His innovation is changing the customary greeting to a religious greeting that is a combination of key words from both Greek and Jewish traditions. These words are *grace* (from the Greek tradition) and *peace* (from the Hebrew tradition).

Make a note card with the words *grace* and *peace* in your choice of lettering style. (As you know, craft stores sell blank greeting cards.) Add your own graphic design. If you wish, write a note inside and mail it right away or save it for another time.

11

The First and Second Letters to the Thessalonians

THE LETTERS AS A UNIT

Why Was the New Testament Written?

THE SHORT ANSWER TO the question, why was the New Testament written? is that Christ did not return. Therefore, it was important to write down the teachings of Jesus as did the writers of the gospels. Paul needed to explain the delay of Christ's return, teach how to live in the present, and help people keep their hopes high. Therefore he wrote 1 Thessalonians.

Scholars are almost equally divided about whether or not Paul wrote 2 Thessalonians.[1] One reason for thinking that someone other than Paul wrote 2 Thessalonians is the omission of Paul's cherished triad of faith, hope, and love.[2] In any case, it is helpful to look at these two books as a unit.

---

1. Brown, *Introduction to the New Testament*, 591.
2. Duling and Perrin, *New Testament*, 263–64.

In addition to having different angles about the delay of Christ's return, these books show different understandings about how to balance joy in the present with yearnings for the fullness of Christ's presence in the future.

FIRST THESSALONIANS: LEAD A LIFE WORTHY OF GOD

The Beginnings of Christian Literature: Paul Writes His First Letter

First Thessalonians is a letter written by Paul in AD 51 or 52 from Corinth. This book is the "earliest complete document" in the New Testament.[3] Paul included Silvanus and Timothy as co-senders. They wrote to the house church in Thessalonica. This city was the capital of the Roman providence of Macedonia, but the culture remained Greek. This detail is important because it explains why Paul in 1 Thes 2:3–8 presents himself as an ideal Greek philosopher who did not act out of greed. Some members of the house church were Jewish in origin, but most were Gentiles, and some had been persecuted by other Gentiles or "compatriots." Paul's overall goal was to help the Thessalonians "lead a life worthy of God" (2:12). His perspective was that it is mandatory to continue loving one another (3:12) and to maintain holiness in personal life (4:1–8).

Line of Thought

In his comforting greeting, Paul and co-senders refer to the church as "in God the Father and the Lord Jesus Christ"

---

3. Harrington, *Who Is Jesus?* 81.

(1:1). He remembers the Thessalonians' work of faith, labor of love, and steadfastness of hope (1:3). He praises the example of the people who, despite persecution, received the gospel with joy (1:6–7). Their turn from pagan worship to the worship of one God had become famous all over Greece. This was a huge change, and many Thessalonians must have lost friends. Paul calls the Thessalonians to standards of personal holiness that serve as missionary examples to all. When Paul and company missed their friends in the church and wondered how they were doing, they sent Timothy to check up on everyone. Timothy returned with the good news of their faith and love (3:6).

Paul is convinced that Christ will return "like a thief in the night," which implies that he will surprise everyone (5:2–4). (Whether the early church's wish for Jesus's return should be taken literally is a matter of debate. Yet certainly there is more to do to actualize the teachings of Jesus. Christian hopes for the future include a world transformed by Jesus's ethic of love and forgiveness.) Life in community is strengthened by helping the weak, seeking to do good rather than repaying evil with evil, rejoicing, praying, and giving thanks (5:14–15).

SECOND THESSALONIANS: EMPOWERMENT FROM THE LOVE OF GOD AND STEADFASTNESS OF CHRIST

The Second Letter to the Thessalonians Continues Discussion: Paul's Friend Helps Paul Address a New Situation

Paul may have written this letter in AD 51 or 52 in Corinth. Or it might have been written at the end of the first century when people were even more concerned about the return of Jesus. I envision the later date and believe that Paul may have written portions of this letter and that a friendly person who understood Paul helped him out when the message became even more relevant.

In 1 Thessalonians Paul emphasized the present aspects of Christian living, which are faith, hope, and love. The new situation that faced the writer of 2 Thessalonians was that the Thessalonians saw evil in the world and experienced fellowship and hope in the present. Therefore they became too certain that Jesus would return soon. Why work if the end is near? Paul gently tells the idlers to work (3:6–14). If Paul had known the present-day hymn, "Work, for the Night is Coming," this hymn would be the pick of the day.

ACTIVITY

Thinking about the Present and the Future

In your church, or in other social situations, do you enjoy fun and fellowship, caring and support? Do you have opportunities to make the world a better place for future generations in your church or outside of the church?

12

The Letter to the Ephesians

Alive Together in Christ

EDITORIAL INTRODUCTION AND EXPANSION OF PAUL'S THINKING

THERE ARE TWO FEATURES of Ephesians that I most want you to remember:

1. The compiler of this letter introduces and expands Paul's thought.
2. The author of Ephesians paints a different picture of the church than is found in the letters that were definitely written by Paul.

Ephesians is a letter that was written in the spirit of Paul. However, in deference to tradition, we will refer to the author as Paul or as the author. Probably written in AD 90 to the saints in Ephesus, Ephesus may have been the place of writing. Three characteristics suggest that Paul was not the author of this letter: The letter was written to a general audience rather than written as Paul did to an individual church.

The sentences in Greek are longer than the sentences Paul wrote.[1] There are developments in the understanding of the church that grew after Paul's founding of churches.

Ephesians as an Editorial Introduction

The author quotes from Paul's letters and sometimes edits out some of Paul's ideas. At other times he expands Paul's thought. He does not talk much about the day of judgment and instead writes about "keeping alert" (6:18) into the on-going future.

In Romans, Paul's solution to the divisions between Jews and Christians in the developing Christian movement is his image of Christians as grafted onto Judaism like a wild olive shoot grafted onto another olive tree (11:17). Therefore, Christians are grafted onto the family tree rooted in Judaism. The author of Ephesians greatly expands Paul's thinking. His faith claim is that through Jesus's death and teachings that eliminated the law, Jesus created a new humanity and peace (2:14–17).

The language of the universality of sin in Eph 2:1–2 is reflective of Paul in Rom 3:9–18. Also, the phrase "clothe yourselves with the new self" (Eph 4:24) is very much like "a new creation is everything" (Gal 6:15).

The Developing and Changing Church

Whereas the church is a loosely organized group of people with various gifts in letters definitely written by Paul, in Ephesians, the gifts are more like institutional job descriptions assigned by Christ (4:11–16). Thus, Christ as the head of the church is a development that goes beyond Paul.

---

1. Duling and Perrin, *New Testament*, 274.

In 1 Corinthians, Paul gives us an up-close picture of an individual church. The author of Ephesians gives us a panoramic picture of the wider or universal church.

UNFOLDING THE LETTER

Following the introduction, the author praises God for grace, redemption, and forgiveness (1:3–7). Paul's prayer is that his readers (and by implication all of us) will know what is the hope to which we are called. A statement of faith follows, proclaiming that all earthly rulers or destructive forces are less powerful than Christ. (1:20–23). Christ is head of the universal church.

The editor rounds out Paul's stress on faith apart from works by saying that we are saved by faith but created for good works (2:8–10). Paul explains his mission to the Gentiles as part of God's plan. He wants us to comprehend the breadth, length, height, and depth of being rooted and grounded in the love of Christ (3:14–19). Such awareness is experience of the fullness of God.

The author says that Ephesians must turn from their lax moral standards. New life in Christ means avoiding hurtful speech and not being greedy. Greed can mean making things into idols or finding material possessions more important than God (5:3–5). Ethics calls for discernment: "Try to find out what is pleasing to the Lord" (5:10). The household code (5:21–23) extends the author's reflection of the church with Christ as head. A good feature to note in our day is that the love of a husband has more weight than wifely submission. Slavery is accepted as a reality of the day. (However, slaves had better lives than slaves in American history.) To my mind, it is appropriate to think about the

Bible as a whole and to stress that some statements in the Bible are not applicable for all times.

ACTIVITY

Introducing Your Friend to the World

Write a paragraph or a short essay to the world introducing a friend who you respect and admire. You may need to interview your friend. In addition to what your friend likes to do, consider including some of your friend's ideas. You may be able to say good things that your friend could not say about him- or herself. You might round out your friend's ideas by saying what those ideas mean to you or why they matter. This will give you a feeling for how the author of Ephesians introduced Paul, promoted his ideas, and updated his readers about the developing church.

PART 4

The Rest of Paul's Letters

13

The Letter to the Galatians

*Bearing One Another's Burdens
Is Fulfilling the Law of Christ*

INVITATION TO INCLUSIVENESS

AT A CHURCH COFFEE hour in a church that my husband served as pastor, an elderly gentleman spoke to me about his conviction that women should not have leadership positions in the church. I quoted from Galatians. "There is no longer Jew or Greek, there is no longer slave or free, there is no longer male and female; for all of you are one in Christ Jesus" (3:28). He replied, "Got me there," and then we enjoyed the coffee hour together in fellowship with our church family.

Call to Christian Freedom

Galatians is a circulating letter and call to Christian freedom. Paul wrote this letter to the churches of Galatia around AD 54–55.[1] This letter was composed to be read aloud to

---
1. Brown, *Introduction to the New Testament*, 468.

each church and was a substitute for Paul's personal presence. The letter defends Paul's understanding of religious requirements.

The Galatians faced an identity crisis. Were they a branch of Judaism? Or were they a new community of Jewish Christians and former Gentile pagans (who did not want to become Jewish before becoming Christians)? Paul's answer was that Gentiles did not have to become Jewish before becoming Christians and thus were exempt from the requirement to be circumcised.

UNFOLDING THE LETTER

Paul was not one of the original disciples, but he saw himself as an apostle (1:1). He was annoyed that people were deserting his more liberal and freeing approach. He asserts that he is not seeking human approval but received his mission to the Gentiles from God (1:6–12), and he recounts his conversion experience (1:13–24). In chapter 2 Paul is especially frustrated with Cephas because Cephas, although a Jew, lived like a Gentile, so why did he back more rigid requirements? Paul expresses his belief that we are justified through faith in Jesus Christ or, as it's sometimes interpreted, by the kind of faith Jesus had in God. Paul shares his belief in chapter 4 that Gentiles are adopted by God. "And because you are children, God has sent the Spirit of his Son into our hearts, crying 'Abba! Father!'"(4:5). Paul sums up the law in chapter 5: "For the whole law is summed up in a single commandment, 'You shall love your neighbor as yourself'" (5:14).

He goes on to say that the fruit of the Spirit is love, joy, peace, patience, kindness, gentleness, and self-control (5:22). Explaining the implications of having the fruit of the

Spirit, he writes, "Bear one another's burdens, and in this way you will fulfill the law of Christ" (6:2). Circumcision is not the issue. A new creation is everything (6:15). "A new creation" echoes Isa 65:17–25 and points to Rev 21:5 and a world that God makes new. Salvation is linked with God's remaking of the world, which people can participate in by bearing one another's burdens. Living in joy and peace and showing gentleness and kindness also help reshape the world. Paul signs his letter with his own hand and prays for the grace of Jesus Christ to be with our spirits.

ACTIVITY

Thinking about the Burdens of Other People

How can you help someone you know or people you do not know bear their burdens? Do you have a problem that you would like to share?

14

The First Letter to the Corinthians

*Faith, Hope, and Love Abide,
and the Greatest of These Is Love*

OVERVIEW

First Corinthians is a letter that is part of a discussion that continues with 2 Corinthians. Paul wrote this letter around AD 54 or 55. He likely wrote from Ephesus[1] to a congregation of mostly Gentile Christians.[2] Paul was away so he had to write to help the church deal with problems and divisions in the emerging church. The most serious division was between rich and poor people (11:17–22). The sacrament we know as Communion, or the Eucharist or the Lord's Supper, was not the same for everyone. The rich ate first and the poor came later. Paul knew that Christian love means equal regard. Basically he told the rich people to eat at home if they were that hungry (11:33).

---

1. Brown, *Introduction to the New Testament*, 512.
2. Harrington, *Who Is Jesus?* 87.

The congregation also argued about what Christians should eat. Paul maintained that Christians could eat meat sacrificed to idols because that pagan practice was meaningless. But if others were upset, the better choice was not to eat the sacrificial meat. His slogan was "'all things are lawful,' but not all things are beneficial" (10:23).

The practice of speaking in tongues presented problems because some people who spoke that way thought they were better than other people. Paul stressed the variety of gifts that people offer to God (12:27–31). The chapter that follows has specific and universal implications. Specifically, people in the Corinthian church will not be boastful about their gifts if they are guided by love. Universally love is an enduring, ongoing virtue.

ARTISTIC FEATURES

Perspective

In the first-century world, death by crucifixion was shameful. Therefore, believing that a crucified person would have had good ideas about how to best live would seem unlikely if not deranged. However Paul believed that Jesus, who was experienced as the risen Christ, was wise and would spiritually lead and guide his followers into the future. Paul's perspective is that Christ crucified is foolishness to the world, but Christ is the source of wisdom (3:18–19).

Texture

Paul writes with texture when he alludes to Old Testament passages. Writing about the resurrection in 1 Cor 15:54–55,

Paul reworks Isa 25:7. Speaking in poetry, Paul wrote: "Death has been swallowed up in victory" and "Where, O death, is your victory?" (15:54–55). Before him, Isaiah wrote: "And he will destroy on this mountain the shroud that is cast over all peoples, the sheet that is spread over all nations; he will swallow up death forever" (Isa 25:7). The first-century listeners to 1 Corinthians might have said, "Ancestors of our Jewish-Christian friends heard something like Paul's faith in the power of love over death before."

Focal Point

The focal point of 1 Corinthians is chapter 13, which is sometimes called the "love chapter." When you look at the focal point of a painting, you may understand how the picture holds together. So it is with 1 Corinthians. Your first introduction to the love chapter may be at a wedding when the pastor or priest reads from this chapter.

Line

Keeping in mind the focal point of Christian love, let us take a walk with Paul's line of thought. Chapters 1–6 are about matters as reported by Chloe's people. In the rest of the book, Paul responds to concerns of his congregation.

Chapter 1

Having heard from Chloe's people that there were divisions in the church, Paul encourages unity of spirit.

Chapter 2

God's wisdom is revealed through the Spirit.

Chapter 3

Paul stresses that he planted, Apollos watered, and God gave growth (v. 6). People in God's field (a metaphor for the church) belong to Christ (vv. 5–9).

Chapter 4

Paul's advice is to not be self-important but be willing to be a fool for Christ.

Chapter 5

Asserting his leadership, Paul speaks out about sexual immorality because immoral behavior destroys community.

Chapter 6

Paul prefers that people in his small church settle disputes among themselves instead of going to court.

Chapter 7

Marriage is good, but Paul prefers the less-encumbered celibate life.

Chapter 8

Paul gives advice to be sensitive to people's feelings about food traditions.

Chapter 9

Paul does not want to be paid for his work, although he does not feel payment is inappropriate for church workers.

Chapter 10

Paul stresses that all things are lawful but not always beneficial (v. 23).

Chapter 11

Head coverings for women and short hair for men are the customs of the day.

Chapter 12

There are varieties of gifts but the same Spirit.

Chapter 13

Paul praises the virtues of love. In this passage the New Testament Greek word for love means Christian love and caring. There are other New Testament words for friendship and romantic love.

Chapter 14

Prophecy has more value than speaking in tongues. Orderly worship includes a hymn, a lesson, a revelation, and speaking in tongues with an interpretation.

Chapter 15

Death does not have the last word (vv. 54–55). By implication, the archenemy, sorrow, does not have the final say either.

Chapter 16

Every week, give to the collection for the Jerusalem church (vv. 1–4). Stand firm in faith, be courageous, and do everything in love (v. 13).

ACTIVITY

Focal Point of Christian Love

Read 13:1–13. This passage is poetic prose. If I have trouble understanding a poem, it is helpful to me to select a phrase that stands out to me or to select a visual image that appeals to me. Sometimes the phrase and visual images are the same but more often they are different. Therefore I invite you to chose a phrase or a visual image in this passage, think about the phrase or image, and if you like, share your reaction with others in your class or in your family.

15

The Second Letter to the Corinthians

In Christ, God Reconciled the World to Godself

OVERVIEW OF A FRAGMENTED LETTER

Second Corinthians is a letter that is a composite of several letters. Paul wrote this letter to the same congregation addressed in 1 Corinthians and all the saints throughout Achaia. Macedonia is likely the place of composition. Its date is AD 54–56. The various understandings of the fragments are very confusing. Rather than going into details, I just want you to know that the letter is fragmented. The basic problem is that Paul is angry. After he wrote 1 Corinthians, Timothy went to Corinth where he found that there were hostile "false apostles" who undermined Paul. Then Paul went to Corinth and was confronted by someone, quite possibly the alleged bad-acting man in 1 Corinthians. Paul went away to cool down and at first thought he should not visit again so he wrote a letter. The Corinthians repented, so Paul did make a third visit.

Paul had to defend his ministry and assert his authority. He had to patch up hurt feelings over his initial failure to visit. His goal was reconciliation. Paul wanted the church people to think well of him and keep on taking the collection for the Jerusalem church.

ARTISTIC FEATURES

Perspective

Paul's perspective is that being united with Christ is the beginning of a new order of creation that offers reconciliation. To my mind, his need to reconcile with his congregation helped him develop his theological understanding of God's reconciliation to the world.

High-Contrast Portraits

Paul paints a detailed picture of himself as an apostle and church leader who is anxious about his charges (11:28). He defends himself by listing his sufferings (11:23–27). In contrast to the more detailed picture of himself, he sketches his opponents (the false apostles) as deceitful (11:3). We do not have their side of the story.

Colorful Words

A colorful slogan that preachers have used over and over that comes from chapter 9, verse 7, is "God loves a cheerful giver."

Untangling a Twisty Line

The line of thought in this book is twisty. The first part is chapters 1–9. In the second part of 2 Corinthians, which is chapters 10–13, the conflict between Paul and the church becomes more intense.

Following the greeting, Paul blesses God as the "God of all consolations" (1:3). Paul says that he can share consolation from God with others because he experienced suffering. Because Paul suffered and experienced consolation from God, he understood pain and therefore says that he could pass on consolation, as could others in his community who felt consoled by God. In Asia, Paul and fellow Christians were so near death that they learned to depend upon God. He says that he at first decided not to visit the Corinthians because he did not want to cause pain. He urges that the offender be shown love so that he will not have overwhelming sorrow (2:7).

Because it is by God's grace that people are engaged in ministry, Paul concludes that they do not lose heart. Paul maintains that he and his followers were afflicted but not crushed, struck down but not destroyed (4:8–9). Paul's working orders were to spread the message of reconciliation between God and humanity, and by implication be reconciled with his congregation. In chapter 7 Paul rejoices in the church's repentance.

Chapter 8 details the first major fundraiser in the Christian church. Paul, whose style is high-sell, wants people to regain enthusiasm for the collection to give to the Jerusalem congregation. However, his perspective on fairness in giving is thoughtful. He seems to clearly know that some people will always have more money than other people have and speaks in terms of fair balance. To paraphrase Paul's textural quotation of the Old Testament passage, Exod 16:18, his vision is that people who have much will not have too much and people with little resources will not have too little (8:14–15).

In the second part of the letter, chapters 10–13, Paul is really angry and goes on quite a tirade about the "false apostles." On a more positive note, Paul has a religious experience and senses Jesus saying to him, "My grace is sufficient for you, for power is made perfect in weakness" (12:8). After going on at length in chapters 12 and 13 about his plan to return to Corinth for a third time, Paul closes his letter and ends with a benediction.

ACTIVITIES

Looking at Art

If you have access to the book *Sister Wendy's 1000 Masterpieces*, look at the painting of Saint Paul by Konrad von Soest.[1] The image, painted around 1400, is a visual statement of Paul's strength in weakness. In addition to looking aggressive, which is the way Saint Paul comes across in 2 Corinthians, he looks defeated, sad, and wounded. Yet there is strength in the saturated colors of red and green in his robe, and in the orange and gold background. These colors may suggest that weakness can be turned into power. The gold background might evoke a hopeful feeling that vulnerable people experience when they are enveloped in the strength of God or human good will at large.

---

1. Beckett, 1000 *Masterpieces*, 246.

Thinking about Strength in Weakness

Sometimes wounded people become healers. Do you know anyone who has had a limitation or personal problem and has turned that problem into a way to help or empower other people?

My personal story is that if I had better driving skills, I would have driven the Girl Scouts to various events or delivered altar flowers from church to people in nursing homes. Because I do not have as much stamina and coordination as many other people, I write. Therefore my limitations have brought out strength to do my best work. Of course, it is my hope that my writing will inform or even inspire other people.

16

The Letter to the Romans

Justification Comes through Faith and Trust

OVERVIEW

THE LETTER TO THE Romans is a letter written by Paul. Unlike his other letters, it does not address a specific problem in a church. This letter was written in Corinth in AD 57–58. Phoebe probably served as postal transportation clerk by delivering the letter to Rome (Rom 16:1).

This well-organized letter has two main parts. The first part is about righteousness through faith. The second part is about the requirements of new life in Christ. Smaller forms within the letter are an opening greeting (1:1–7), a prayer of thanksgiving (1:8–15), a statement of theme (1:16–17), travel plans (15:22–23), and a conclusion (chapter 16).

When pared down and summarized, there is linear logic to Paul's letter. However, Romans is challenging and can be tiring to read because you can feel Paul's exhausting struggle to deal with what he owes to his Jewish heritage. Of course, he wanted everyone to follow him into the Christian movement, but that did not happen. In brief, Paul concluded that the reason that not all Jews accepted the Christian movement is a mystery (11:25) and that God did not forsake God's people, the Jews (11:1–2).

ARTISTIC ELEMENTS

Lens

Paul's lens is justification by faith. This is a complicated idea. It can mean that a person is justified by faith in Christ or by having the kind of trust that Jesus had in his heavenly Father.

The word *justification* is related to justice. To enormously simplify the concept, N. T. Wright argues that Romans 1:17 (which states that the one who is righteous will live by faith) is about covenant faithfulness and justice.[1] The covenant was with Israel, but when the covenant was extended to Gentiles, they would know what its "own life was about."[2] In biblical days, people of faith, who were bound together in their covenanted life, understood that not all justice flowed from Rome. Justification is related to reconciliation. When you have faith, trust, and understanding about what matters, you will likely feel reconciled to God or to the universe.

---

1. *New Interpreter's Bible*, 10:403.
2. *New Interpreter's Bible*, 10:405.

Words that Color Paul's Letter[3]

- *death*: A punishment for sin and also a power that goes with sin and the law
- *faith*: Total trust in God, demonstrated by Abraham. "Faith in Christ" many connote the trust Jesus had in God or faith in Christ as a personal example or savior.
- *flesh*: The part of a person that is angry with God, and a rebellious attitude that is opposite of spirit.
- *Gentile*: Non-Jews and also sometimes Gentile Christians
- *gospel*: The good news of Jesus the Christ and what his living, death, and resurrection opened up for all people. In brief, the gospel for Paul is "the power of God for salvation to everyone who has faith" (Rom 1:16).
- *justification*: Even before the Last Judgment, justification means that God's acquittal—which suggests clearance or a clean slate—makes righteousness possible. Again, *reconciliation* is close in meaning.
- *law*: Usually the Mosaic law or sometimes natural law, which is the natural ability of people to know right from wrong. For Paul, Mosaic law was good, but it told people what sin is and thus tempted them to not always do right.

---

3. The following definitions are based on the section "Paul's Theological Vocabulary" in Harrington, *Romans*, 12–15.

- *salvation*: Rescue from moral evil in the present
- *sin*: Wrongdoing, or a strong power linked with death or basic alienation from God
- *spirit*: Openness to God in interior places that are touched by the Holy Spirit
- *world*: Sometimes the world is seen as neither good nor bad, but at other times it is seen as under the power of sin.

Texture

The poem in chapter 3, verses 10–18 alludes to passages in the Old Testament to show that sin is widespread and that in Paul's understanding everyone needs the gospel. Here are some of the ties:

- Rom 3:10 reflects Eccl 7:20.
- Rom 3:11 echoes Ps 14:2–3.
- Rom 15–17 shares concerns with Isa 59:7–8.

Linear Logic

There are two main parts in Romans. Part 1, chapters 1–11, is a sustained argument for the idea that the only way to satisfy God's demands for righteousness is through faith. Part 2, chapters 12–16, is an explanation of the requirements of Christian living. Discover Paul's linear logic in a chapter-by-chapter consideration of the text.

Part 1: Righteousness through Faith

Chapter 1

The gospel reveals the righteousness of God for every believer, first the Jews, then the Greeks. Righteousness of God is revealed through faith (vv. 16–17). Gentiles knew God through nature, but they ignored God and did not always behave well. Thus failure to acknowledge God can be the root of sin.

Chapter 2

God does not show partiality and judges according to actions (vv. 6–11). (There is a hint of universalism here.)

Chapter 3

God entrusted his oracles to the Jews, but God is God for everyone. The law could not do for Paul what Christ did, but it was an important witness. All people have sinned but are justified by faith apart from works prescribed by the law (v. 28), or are justified by a radical trust in God, whether or not they have been circumcised or have kept the law. (To reiterate: "faith" can mean the faith, faithfulness, and trust of Christ, as well as faith in Christ.)

Chapter 4

Abraham trusted God, and his faith, as radical trust, even before circumcision, made him righteous.

Chapter 5

Christ died and lived for us. Reconciliation came from Christ's death, and salvation from his living. "For if while we were enemies, we were reconciled to God through the death of his Son, much more surely, having been reconciled, we will be saved by his life" (v. 10). (Humanists as well as Christians can testify to finding meaning, direction, and wholeness or salvation through following Jesus's teachings.)

Chapter 6

Our baptism into Christ's death and resurrection means that sin and death no longer are in control. Walking in newness of life is about the future resurrected life as well as new life in the present.

Chapter 7

Sin is part of the human condition that prevents us from being our best, unified selves. Paul questions the validity of the rules that made him aware of sin. The Spirit gave him new life.

Chapter 8

The law of the Spirit gives life and sets people free (v. 2). People who are led by the Spirit are children of God (v. 14). Yearnings for the fullness of God were so pervasive that the universe groaned in waiting (v. 22). Nothing can separate us from the love of God (vv. 35–39).

Chapter 9

Being children of God depends upon promise and election not just biological heritage. Christ is like a master potter (v. 21).

Chapter 10

Christ is the "end" of the law in the sense of its "fulfillment" (v. 4). Faith in the heart means that God is near and salvation is at hand (v. 9). There is no distinction between Jew and Greek because the same Lord generously responds to everyone's prayers (vv. 9–13).

Chapter 11

Paul does not deny his Jewish heritage but sees Jewish Christians as the faithful remnant who providentially respond to Jesus and show that Gentiles can enjoy full membership in the family of God. God has not ultimately rejected Israel. God has grafted Gentiles onto the family tree (vv. 23–24). God's call to Israel is irrevocable (v. 29).

Part 2: The Requirements of New Life in Christ

Chapter 12

New life in Christ means renewal, discerning the will of God, participating in the body of Christ by modestly sharing spiritual gifts, persevering in prayer, loving the genuine, practicing hospitality, blessing those who persecute you, and showing concern for enemies (vv. 1–20). "Do not be overcome by evil. But overcome evil with good" (v. 21).

Chapter 13

Love fulfills the law (v. 8), so pay taxes and fulfill the law through loving your neighbor as yourself. (The government at the time was fairly friendly, so of course Paul advised civil obedience. By the time the book of Revelation was written, the authorities were hostile.)

Chapter 14

In contrast to harshly judging others, pursue peace and mutual building up of communities. The kingdom of God, a concept that Paul rarely uses, is about righteousness, peace, and joy in the Holy Spirit (v. 17). Pursue those things that please neighbors and make for peace.

Chapter 15

Paul prays for harmony. He asks that church members welcome one another as Christ welcomed them so that all Gentiles might glorify the God of hope and mercy (vv. 7–9).

Chapter 16

Paul's final greeting acknowledges the contributions of a lively group of men and women.

ACTIVITIES

Thinking about Atonement

The most basic definition of *atonement* is what the word suggests when broken into parts: *at-one-ment*. Religiously speaking, atonement means "at one with God." Paul talks about atonement in 3:25. Theologians have written tomes about various theories of atonement. Some believe that Jesus's death was a ransom for our sins. Another related angle is that Jesus served as a scapegoat that bares the blame for others. One of my college professors, Dr. Lawrence Meredith, said that Jesus's sacrificial death on the cross means that animal sacrifices were no longer necessary. Still others, like my more liberal college professor, Dr. John L. Cheek, suggested that Jesus's example of teaching and sacrificial death saves people by showing them how to live. My personal belief is that Jesus died to open up ethical monotheism to non-Jews, which is belief in one God who is righteous and just. Reconciliation and peace can come from acceptance, from forgiveness when asking for it, and from learning through Jesus's teachings how to ethically navigate life. However you understand atonement, when you feel reconciled, accepted, and at one with God, it is more possible to embrace the promise of God's abiding presence given in Rom 8:31–39. These verses may be Paul's most important words. Sometimes Romans is nicknamed the "Gospel according to Paul."

Embracing the Promise of Romans 8

When I was a senior in high school, an unusual number of classmates lost a parent in death. With each sympathy note, I included verses from Romans 8, selecting verses 31, 35, and 37-39. Please read these verses.

Art Project

Make a collage of pictures of faces that symbolize God's grace and therefore help you have faith. (A collage is anything glued to paper or board.) Think about the faces of people who suggest love, patience, faithfulness, concern, acceptance, welcome, and understanding. You may want to include a picture of Christ as well as anyone who helps you feel that nothing can separate you from the love of God. If you prefer, reflect on the possibilities of love arising from a source of caring deep in the genetic markings of human beings.

17

The Letter to Philemon

Christian Love Kindles Kindred Bonds

Alliteration is a good way to remember the main idea of this book. Philemon is a phenomenal picture of the city of Philadelphia, which in New Testament Greek means "brotherly or sisterly love."

OVERVIEW

While in prison in AD 55, Paul wrote this letter to Philemon. He may have written it from Ephesus.[1] He requested freedom for a runaway slave named Onesimus. We can assume that Paul's request was honored, or we would not likely have the story about Paul, Philemon, and Onesimus in the New Testament.

---

1. Brown, *Introduction to the New Testament*, 503.

SUMMARY OF THE STORY

Not only is Philemon a letter, it is also a moving story. Martin Luther said it gives us a tender illustration of Christian love.[2] Onesimus is in prison with Paul. He serves Paul and Paul converts him. Paul wants to send Onesimus back not as a slave but as a brother to Philemon and also wants Philemon to free Onesimus. So Paul writes a tactful letter appealing on the basis of love. In case Onesimus did something wrong, Paul covers all the bases by telling Philemon to charge his own account. Raymond E. Brown says that Paul's request challenged Philemon to defy convention.[3] New life in Christ empowered Paul and Philemon to do the right thing.

I heard a story from my college professor, John L. Cheek, who heard it from his graduate school professor, Edgar J. Goodspeed, who heard it from professors before him. The story continues to be reported as possibly being true. Raymond E. Brown said that forty or fifty years after Paul wrote Philemon, Ignatius, the bishop of Antioch, wrote a letter to the Ephesian church and had much to say about their bishop named Onesimus. Onesimus, the former slave, may have become a bishop.

ARTISTIC FEATURES

Perspective

Paul's perspective was that in Christ, people are all brothers and sisters.

---

2. *New Interpreter's Bible*, 11:886 cites Eduard Lohse, *Colossians and Philemon*, 188; Lohse, in turn, cites Martin Luther on Philemon.

3. Brown, *Introduction to the New Testament*, 506.

Focal Point

The focal point is love in action, or as Paul put it, "all the good that we may do for Christ" (Phlm 6).

ACTIVITIES

Looking at Art

If you have access to Phaidon Press's *Art Book*, please go to page 391 and look at *Madonna and Child between Two Angels* (1475–80) by Luca della Robbia. This image can symbolize inclusive Christian fellowship with Jesus and Mary as central figures.[4]

Creating Your Own Art

Using a compass or tracing a dish, draw a circle on any size of paper. Paste your own designs or cut out pictures of flowers, leaves, fruit, or any decorative image you want. In the middle, put a picture of your choice. You might consider a picture of your church, Mary and Jesus, or people engaged in social action. The decorative circle will symbolize welcome and inclusivity. Fruits can suggest the fruits of the spirit. Whatever is inside the circle will be a focal point.

---

4. Phaidon Press, *Art Book*, 391.

18

The Letter to the Philippians

*Let the Same Mind Be in You
that Was in Christ Jesus*

OVERVIEW

PHILIPPIANS IS A LETTER with the customary greeting, body, and closing benediction. In contrast to the calm reasoning in Romans, Paul wrote this letter with warmth, affection, and prayerful movement. While Paul in Romans is a theologian, in Philippians he is like a pastoral counselor leading a prayer service or retreat in which participants identify their best kinds of service. The letter may be a compilation of letters. It was written around AD 56 and no one knows where for sure. Philippi was a Roman colony of about ten thousand people. Paul's converts there were almost all from families of Gentile origin.[1]

---

1. *New Interpreter's Bible*, 11:469–71 by Morna D. Hooker.

ARTISTIC FEATURES

Perspective

Christians participate in Christ by following his example of obedience and humble service. The idea of living like Christ is woven throughout the New Testament and comes to fullest expression in Philippians.

Color Word

The word *joy* colors the text. Paul remembers the Philippians with joy (1:4). Even though he is in prison, Paul rejoices and believes in his future deliverance (1:18–19). He anticipates the Philippians' continued progress and joy in faith (1:25). Towards the end of his letter Paul calls his brother and sisters his joy and crown (4:1) and advises rejoicing in the Lord (4:4).

Focal Point

Two words, *essence* and *exaltation*, express the core of Paul's thought in Philippians. The historical Jesus's essence was service to God. In Paul's understanding, Jesus as the risen Christ and Lord is exaltation.

Prayerful Movement in Text

Writing from prison, Paul greets the saints in Philippi. He tells them of his joyful prayers for them. One of his prayers is that their love may overflow more and more with knowledge and full insight (1:3–9). Paul wants his flock to know that his imprisonment helped spread the gospel because even the imperial guard took note (1:12–13). Building upon his earlier prayer, Paul asks that people live in a manner worthy of the gospel and that they be in one spirit (1:27).

In chapter 2, Paul asks the Philippians to make his joy complete by having unity of mind and love. Unity here does not refer to intellectual thought but to having a common attitude. (To fast forward to today, emulating the mind of Christ may be more important than your exact beliefs about him. Christians of many kinds and humanists can discuss what it means to think and respond like Jesus.) In a hymn inserted into his letter, Paul delivers his most important message of Christian humility and service saying:

> Let the same mind be in you that was in Christ Jesus, who, though he was in the form of God, did not regard equality with God, as something to be exploited, but emptied himself, taking the form of a slave, being born in human likeness. And being found in human form, he humbled himself and became obedient to the point of death—even death on a cross. Therefore God also highly exalted him and gave him the name that is above every name, so that at the name of Jesus every knee should bend, in heaven and on earth and under the earth, and every tongue should confess that Jesus Christ is Lord, to the glory of God the Father. (2:5–11)

Following the hymn, Paul instructs his people about living to the glory of God. "Shining like stars" in the darkness of the world (2:15) is a metaphor that echoes Jesus's teachings about being the light of the world (Matt 5:14). Paul rejoices that Epaphroditus has recovered from an almost fatal illness (2:25–30).

In chapter 3, Paul makes it clear that his values have changed from faith in the Mosaic law (3:6) to faith in

Christ's fidelity to his Father (3:9–11). Using an athletic image, Paul states, "I press on toward the goal for the prize of the heavenly call of God in Christ Jesus" (3:14). Then, using a political image that his readers would understand, Paul tells his them that they are citizens of heaven (3:20) as well as earth.

Winding down his prayerful letter Paul urges Euodia and Syntyche to be of the same mind in the Lord, in a dispute long forgotten. He says, "Rejoice in the Lord always; again I will say 'Rejoice'" (4:4). "And the peace of God, which surpasses all understanding, will guard your hearts and your minds in Christ Jesus" (4:7). He advises thinking about whatever is true, honorable, just, and pure (4:8). Closing in benediction, he says," The grace of the Lord Jesus Christ be with your spirit" (4:23).

ACTIVITY

Shining Like Stars

Paul asked his readers to shine like stars in the world (Phil 2:15). Similarly, Jesus said in Matt 5:14, "You are the light of the world." There are many forms of service and different ways to shine. Praying for others, helping your parents with a younger sibling, and serving in your church's youth mission project are some of the ways to shine. Doing your best in school increases your chances of discovering your best gifts. Your best kind of service can be a joy for others and for yourself. Perhaps you write for a school newspaper and are concerned for truth or volunteer in a library and therefore support knowledge and the humanities, which are God's auxiliaries. How do you give back to life or shine to the glory of God? Whatever your form of service, you are a star shining in the world.

You Are a Star Today

Draw a free form star or a star from a pattern with black marker, or use the star designs that are at the end of this chapter. If you own the book, of course, you are free to color in your book. The designs in this book are by my daughter Amy Elizabeth Chace. Feel free to photocopy as many times as you would like for yourself or others. You might want to write your name on a star. Add your own colors with markers, paint, or colored pencils.

PART 5

Christ Served by Growing Ministry

19

The Letter to the Colossians

Christ Is the Wisdom of God

OVERVIEW

COLOSSIANS IS A LETTER with a prison setting that was probably written in Paul's name by a disciple addressing Gentile Christians in Colossae. These Christians were members of a church that was not founded by Paul. This letter was written in Ephesus no later than AD 80 and maybe earlier.

Paul's disciple (hereafter called the author, the writer, or Paul as a namesake) warned Gentile Christians against the dangers of teachers who seem to have endorsed a form of esoteric Judaism that emphasized fasting and visionary experiences. Paul addresses a very specific form of Judaism and should not be seen as condemning all forms of Judaism or ascetic practices. He urges his audience to practice virtues such as compassion, kindness, and patience (3:8–12). Paul finds wisdom personified in Christ.

ARTISTIC FEATURES

Color

Six words introduce and summarize Colossians. These six words, in three phrases, are: (1) colossal church, (2) cosmic Christ, and (3) congregational chorus.

- *colossal church*: In this letter, the church is becoming a more structured institution. Eventually, the organized institution will be a colossal church with Christ as the head.
- *cosmic Christ*: Christ is seen as the true representative of God. The body of Christ is not just the church but a cosmic reality (1:18, 24; 2:19; 3:15).
- *congregational chorus*: In time, many churches will be a worldwide congregational chorus affirming the Christ hymn in Colossians (1:15–20).

Perspective

The author's perspective is that Christ is the full embodiment of God and "in him all things hold together" (1:17).

Focal Point

The focal point of this book is a metaphor derived from the text: Christ as cosmic glue. Wisdom in Christ holds all things together. Faith can be an adhesive that binds community together.

A LETTER IN TWO PARTS

Part 1: Theological Statements

Paul greets the saints in Colossae. Finding richness in Judaism, the author expands upon a familiar motif of personified wisdom. Drawing upon Prov 8 and Sir 24, Paul finds wisdom in Christ, who holds all things together like glue. In the Colossian hymn, Christ is the image of the invisible God, existing before anything else (1:18).

The writer wants people to remain true to the faith that they had been taught. He assures his people that Christian life should not be reduced to austere practices or worship of angels (2:2–19).

Part 2: Ethics

New life in Christ means being clothed in virtues of "compassion, kindness, humility, gentleness and patience" (3:12) and showing mutual respect in human relationships. Devotion to prayer is a good thing (4:2). Speech to outsiders should be appropriate for the listeners (4:6). In the spirit of Paul, the author gives a benediction: "Grace be with you" (4:18).

ACTIVITY

Hope on the Horizon

Think about the lovely phrase, "Hope laid up for you in heaven" (1:5) and the themes in 1:3–8. These themes include the practice of thanking God, the importance of faith and hope in Christian life, and hope as the horizon for Christian existence.[1] Each of these themes can be realized through daily habits.

Draw a line on a piece of paper. Write the word "hope" on the line. Think about people or programs that inspire hope for you personally, for the future of your faith community, or for the future of the earth. Sketch images or jot down phrases. Keep these words and images for future use or use them right away in a picture, essay, or poem.

---

1. Harrington, *Paul's Prison Letters*, 84.

20

The Letter of James

Be God's Friends by Being Doers of the Word

OVERVIEW

JAMES RESEMBLES A SERMON or homily in letter form. Yet, James is better understood as a wisdom instruction.[1] James, like other ancient writings, is concerned with "the practical wisdom of right behavior."[2] One estimated date for the book of James is AD 80–90, if this letter is written in the name of James, as most scholars conclude.[3] The author of James was a conservative Jewish Christian who was very loyal to observing the law. Older ways of being holy that include attention to the first five books of the Bible, known as Torah, continued to help James's community draw close to God, as Jesus did through purity, piety, and prayer.

1. Harrington, *Who Is Jesus?* 159.
2. *New Interpreter's Bible*, 12:179.
3. Brown, *Introduction to the New Testament*, 726.

This letter was written somewhere in the eastern Mediterranean world to a general audience. The wisdom in this book is so universal that it feels contemporary and applicable to both people who believe in God and to people who are humanists. The address to "the twelve tribes" (1:1) may not be literal but rather address Christians who were loyal to the heritage of Israel.[4] The first Christians to hear this letter appreciated their Jewish roots and could easily understand Jesus as the wise teacher portrayed in the book of Matthew. For example, Jesus's teachings on our relationship to worldly possessions are similar in James and Matthew. In James 4:4, James wrote that "friendship with the world is enmity towards God." Likewise, Matthew wrote in Matt 6:24 that "you cannot serve God and wealth."

ARTISTIC FEATURES

Perspective

The perspective of James is that religion has practical applications. Getting along with others is important. Wisdom is open to reason and bears the fruit of mercy and kindly deeds.

Texture

James drew upon the Old Testament book of Leviticus, a source that Matthew also used: "You shall not take vengeance or bear a grudge against any of your people, but you shall love your neighbor as yourself" (Lev 19:18). In some ways, James is an exploration and elaboration of the many implications of Lev 19:18. Like Matthew, James is concerned with Jesus as fulfillment of the law. To James, loving one's

---

4. Brown, *Introduction to the New Testament*, 739.

neighbor as oneself is the royal law (2:8) and doing well means fulfilling the royal law.

Counterbalancing Themes

James is about work that flows from faith. The book of Romans is about faith that can fuel work. Therefore the emphasis on faith in Romans and emphasis on work in James counterbalance and enrich the other.

Use of Line Contrasts with Line in Romans

James and Romans have different styles of line. Romans is written in a straight, logical line. James is more emotionally composed of pearls of wisdom. The individual pearls are like little sermons that make one longer sermon about friendship with God. The golden clasp, which defines religion and holds the necklace together, is found in chapter 1, verse 27. This verse states that pure religion is caring for orphans and widows in distress.

Line of the Text, or Pearls on the Necklace

Trials Lead to Perfection

James asks readers to remain steadfast under persecution. Trials develop character and fortitude (1:2–4). Ask God in prayer for wisdom as you grow (1:5). Humanists, who do not pray to God, might imagine a conversation with a wise and understanding person. Even if you believe in God, as I do, sometimes imagining a conversation helps one to uncover new thoughts or answers. Once a pastor asked me in a guided meditation to imagine a person and talk with him or her. I decided to talk to a compassionate editor and by the end of the guided meditation I had edited my thoughts and feelings and discovered fresh insights.

Tempting Ourselves

Some personal trials come from feelings inside us and not from God. People tempt themselves (1:12-15).

"Be Doers of the Word"

Doers will be blessed in their doing. The golden clasp (Jas 1:27) defines faith in action. The clasp of a necklace holds the necklace together like service projects that hold faith communities together.

Practice What You Preach

Do not show partiality to the rich (2:1-13). Financially poor people can be spiritually rich. Loving our neighbors as ourselves is the royal law (2:8).

Dead Works

"Faith without works is dead" (2:14-17). James cites the good work of Rahab, who was a righteous Gentile who helped the Hebrews. See Josh 2:1-24 for this story, which shows that females can be action heroes.

Words Matter

Words can both bless and curse (3:9-10). We can use words to hurt people, so watch what you say.

Sowing Peace

Get rid of bitterness and envy (3:13-14). Selfish ambition is not spiritual wisdom. Real wisdom from above is pure, peaceful, and gentle (vv. 16-17).

Draw Near to God

If you draw near to God, God will draw near to you. Be friends with God, and God will be friends with you.

Judge Not

Envy can result in slander and sanctimonious judgment of neighbors (4:11–12). So do not let envy turn you into a person who is nasty or mean-spirited.

ACTIVITY

Pure and Strong Religion

Both clasps on necklaces and buckles on belts hold things together. Pure and strong religion holds faith communities together. Draw a clasp or buckle or use the drawings at the end of this chapter. Color or add your own details and write out the words from Jas 1:27 on your paper.

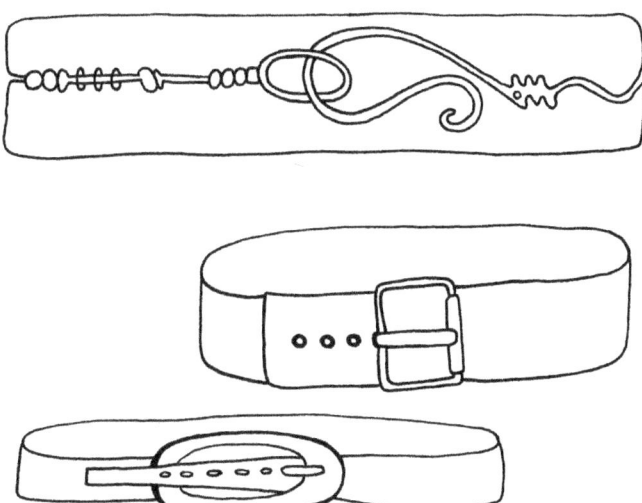

21

The First and Second Letters to Timothy, and the Letter to Titus

Guard the Faith

OVERVIEW OF 1 TIMOTHY, 2 TIMOTHY, AND TITUS

First Timothy, 2 Timothy, and Titus are called the Pastoral Letters because the authors are concerned about pastoral care, church organization, and preservation of beliefs.

Paul or the leader writing in his name is a pastor to pastors. Traditionally called Paul, the author tells Timothy and Titus how to be good pastors who have inner lives to match how they look in public. These letters also summarize beliefs and explain church structures in a male-dominated society.

God and Christ are equally described as "Savior." Two faith statements are found in 1 Tim 2:3-6 and Titus 2:11-14.

FIRST TIMOTHY: SET YOUR HEART AND HOPES ON GOD

Clergy Manual

This book resembles a clergy manual describing proper behavior for church leaders. An unknown author, who used words that were not in Paul's vocabulary,[1] wrote this letter in Paul's name. He wrote to Timothy, who was a good pastor in contrast to other leaders with issues that belong to their time and place. The majority of scholars estimate the date of composition as toward the end of the first century.[2] In addition to wanting church leaders to behave well according to the standards of the time, the author did not want any different doctrines taught.

Themes and Theological Concerns Shape the Text

Universal in the Particular

The author gives instructions about clergy behavior and etiquette for people in the church of his day. Two general concerns have implications for Christians throughout the centuries. The first goal of instruction is to share "love that comes from a pure heart, a good conscience, and sincere faith" (1:5). The second truth with broad implications is that it is better to set one's hopes on God than on "the uncertainty of riches" (6:17).

---

1. Duling and Perrin, *New Testament*, 486.
2. Brown, *Introduction to the New Testament*, 654.

Place of Money

Timothy is advised to be content with enough because the desire for excessive riches can lead to ruin.

Paul and Herald of Truth

Paul is called a "herald" of truth (2:7). The basic differences between him and the false teachers are not clear; however, those teachers do forbid marriage and abstain from certain foods (4:1–5).

Leadership Guidelines

The author sketches the qualifications of deacons and bishops, who should be temperate, gentle, and respectful (3:2). The bishop should "manage his household," a metaphor for the church, and be "well thought of by outsiders" (3:7). Women are told to be modest in dress and not teach men (2:11). Teaching men possibly refers to bossing husbands around in public.

Prayers and Cares

The author tells Timothy to pray for people in high places, to live a quiet life (2:2), and to follow the guidelines for taking care of widows who are truly in need (6:17–19). The author also warns Timothy to guard the teachings of the church that have been entrusted to him (6:20).

SECOND TIMOTHY: BE WILLING TO SHARE IN SUFFERING AND PURSUE RIGHTEOUSNESS, FAITH, LOVE, AND PEACE

A Letter of Continuity of Faith

Second Timothy is a letter. Probably written in Rome[3] by a sympathetic commentator, it is very true to Paul's spirit. We will call him Paul.

Artistic Features

Focal Point

The focal point is continuity of faith. Paul cites the faith of Timothy's mother and grandmother (1:5), and he hopes that Timothy will rekindle his inner gift of warming faith and service (1:6).

Line of Thought

Paul wants Timothy to maintain the standard teachings (1:13). Speaking from the heart of Pauline theology, the author proclaims that God saves us not according to works but according to grace, which was given in Christ Jesus (1:9).

Timothy is encouraged to "be strong in the grace that is in Christ Jesus" (2:1) and to "share in suffering like a good soldier of Christ Jesus" (2:3). The author advises Timothy to shun youthful passions and pursue righteousness, faith, love, and peace (2:22).

---

3. Brown, *Introduction to the New Testament*, 673.

Making his final confession, Paul says, "I have fought the good fight, I have finished the race, I have kept the faith" (4:7).

TITUS:
LIVE GODLY LIVES FOR THE SAKE OF THE FAITH

A Letter for the Sake of the Faith

Titus is a letter to Titus that was most likely written in the name of Paul at the end of the first century or the start of the second century.[4] Titus may have been in Crete, and the author may have written from Ephesus. Paul, as he is traditionally called, focused on doctrine and steadfastness.

Texture and Text

As you know, texture provides continuity. Paul applies the Old Testament concept of being a servant to himself. (See 2 Sam 7:5 and Jer 7:25.) Thus the understanding of being servants of God has a long history, flowing from the Hebrew Scriptures into the New Testament and onward into our contemporary world.

Titus is told to appoint elders (1:5). Bishops should not be arrogant and quick-tempered. They should be devout and hospitable (1:7–8). The most serious accusation against false teachers is that "they deny [God] by their actions" (1:16). Temperance, prudence, and soundness of faith were virtues (2:1–2) then and now. Titus is told to teach sound doctrine (2:1). In the spirit of the day, women are told to be submissive and therefore commend themselves to the society of the

---

4. Ibid., 639.

day (2:5). The author honors Pauline heritage and stresses Paul's conviction of salvation by faith (3:5). In a spirit of counterbalance, he goes on to say that good works meet real needs and keep people productive (3:5–8).

ACTIVITY

For Your Consideration

Do you deny God by your actions? Conversely, do you affirm God by your actions? Please do not feel you must share your thoughts with others. Just think about these questions.

Part 6

Christians in Trouble

22

The First Letter of Peter

If Persecuted, Be Culturally Conservative and Confidently Cast Your Cares upon God

OVERVIEW OF 1 PETER

FIRST PETER IS A general letter to a cluster of churches written in the name of Peter between AD 80 and 90.[1] We will call the writer Peter. Within the letter there are household codes, hymn fragments, and allusions to sayings from the Sermon on the Mount, perhaps from sources earlier than the Gospels. The author is like a combined coach and cheerleader. He wrote to Christians, most of whom were not Jews first.[2] Peter wanted to give Christians strength to live in a hostile land and find meaning in suffering.

THE COMMUNITY OF PETER

People in the community of Peter felt like aliens. Feeling like strangers may have been symbolic or they may have literally

1. Harrington, *Who Is Jesus?* 164–65.
2. Ibid., 167.

experienced persecution under Nero, or local persecution under Domitian.[3] These people may have been on the margins of society like migrant workers or they may have been alienated because of their beliefs. In any case, prospects of social or political persecution were in the air. Peter's people did not feel at home in the world. If Rome was actively persecuting the community of Peter, Peter would not likely have urged his flock to honor the emperor. But they had to be careful.

CONTINUING CONSOLATION FOR CHRISTIANS

Peter guides his community and future readers towards a blessed spiritual life. Three theological convictions that support trust in the goodness of God are:

1. Through the resurrection of Jesus we have a new birth into a living hope (1:3)
2. Faith like gold is refined by fire (1:7)
3. Belief leads to rejoicing with glorious joy (1:8)

A TEXT OF LIVING HOPE

In this letter, living hope flows from formation of Christian identity, to witness in a pagan world, and finally to ethical behavior even when persecuted.

Identity

Peter's statement of new identity is "Blessed be the God and Father of our Lord Jesus Christ! By his great mercy he has given us a new birth into a living hope through the resurrec-

---

[3]. Duling and Perrin, *New Testament*, 476.

tion of Jesus Christ from the dead" (1:3). Quoting Leviticus, Peter reminds his readers that God is holy and calls us to be holy (1:16). Therefore, holiness is a mark of identity.

Witness

Honorable deeds and good conduct are witness. "Conduct yourselves honorably among the Gentiles, so that, though they malign you as evildoers, they may see your honorable deeds and glorify God when he comes to judge" (2:12). Because cultural conservatism does not stand out as subversive, it is a form of protection.

Ethics

Speaking in the spirit of Jesus, Peter says, "Finally, all of you, have unity of spirit, sympathy, love for one another, a tender heart, and a humble mind. Do not repay evil for evil or abuse for abuse; but, on the contrary, repay with a blessing" (3:8–9). (The community of Peter knew evil in society. Pastors need to stress that the social ethic of responding to abuse with a blessing does not sanction domestic violence.)

Church leaders should tend their flocks like the chief shepherd (5:4) who is Christ. In suffering, entrust yourself to God. Cast your cares upon God (5:7).

ACTIVITY

Considering Christians and Culture

Every person has to decide how to relate to culture. Is there anything in our society that you question?

23

The Letter of Jude

Freedom in Christ Does Not Mean Exemption from Moral Authority

OVERVIEW

Jude is a very short, opinionated letter. No one knows for sure when it was written. Estimated dates range from AD 50 to 100.[1] Either Jesus's youngest brother or a younger spiritual brother wrote it. In either case, writing it was a brotherly labor of love. Palestine was a place where Jesus's brothers were well remembered, so the letter might have been written in Palestine. Jude writes with pastoral concern "to those who are called, and beloved in God and kept safe for Jesus Christ" (v. 1). Jude's perspective is that freedom in Christ does not mean exemption from moral standards.

---

1. Brown, *Introduction to the New Testament*, 749.

TEXT

The line of thought in Jude is that the faithful need to "contend for the faith" (v. 3) by making sure that new life in Christ is not perverted into doing anything regardless of consequences. Some people blemished the community by being concerned only for themselves and turning the love feast into a big party (v. 12). If you were the brother or sister of Jesus, wouldn't you want your community to remain pure and holy?

ACTIVITY

Practice Discernment

Jude uses varied images to describe the teachers who taught that freedom in Christ meant that just about anything goes. Consider the phrase "wild waves of the sea, casting up the foam of their own shame" (v. 13). Is destructive behavior such as "road rage" or speech that disregards the feelings of others and thus results in a metaphorical frothing of the mouth ever a perversion of Christian freedom? Is lawless behavior ever a result of a sense of shame from feeling worthless and having nothing to lose by hurtful behavior? If people can believe, like Jude, that they are loved by God, then they will not feel like nobodies.

For those who do not believe in God as well as for those who do, affirmation of the value of each individual may help one embrace one's own intrinsic worth.

24

The Second Letter of Peter

Wait Patiently for New Heavens and a New Earth, Where Righteousness Is at Home

OVERVIEW

Second Peter is a homily or meditation in the form of a letter, and an expansion upon Jude, which is quoted but not acknowledged as a source.[1] The author of 2 Peter is not the author of 1 Peter, but like the writer of 1 Peter, he followed the literary practice of writing a final message for another person. The date of composition is AD 130, give or take a decade.[2] The readers of this letter, which might have been written in Rome, were a general audience in the eastern Mediterranean area where people knew Paul's writings and the writings of 1 Peter.[3]

---

1. Brown, *Introduction to the New Testament*, 761.
2. Ibid., 762.
3. Ibid., 762.

TEXT

After his greeting, the author says that through the knowledge of Christ, who has called us by his own glory and goodness (1:3) we "may become participants of the divine nature" (1:4). Virtues that are part of participating in God include self-control, endurance with godliness, and mutual affection with love (1:5–7). Writing as Peter would have spoken, the author advises hopefulness until "the morning star rises in your hearts" (1:19). In chapter 2, the author ups the ante in criticizing the false teachers he says are "trained in greed" (2:14) and "slaves to whatever masters them" (2:19). In chapter 3, the author's perspective is that "with the Lord one day is like a thousand years" (2:8). Waiting for Christ's return, the author says, "we wait for new heavens and a new earth, where righteousness is at home" (3:13).

ACTIVITY

Literary and Artistic Exploration

The dawn of a new day with "the morning star rises in your hearts" (2 Pet 1:19) is an evocative metaphor. In historical context, the "rising star" referred to the return of Christ. To individualize this image, think about how whenever the love of Christ rises within you, there is a little earthly second coming. Perhaps you could paint a picture or write a poem or essay about a time when a spirit of compassion, hope for the future, or concern for world justice rose up in your mind.

PART 7

Jesus as Helper,
and Christ as the Risen Lord

25

The Letter to the Hebrews

*Reflect on Christ the High Priest
and Continue in Faithfulness*

OVERVIEW

Introducing the Author

THE AUTHOR OF THE Letter to the Hebrews and place of its composition are not known with certainty. The church father Origen said that only God knows who wrote Hebrews.[1] However, we do know some things about the author. He understood Judaism, wrote superb Greek, and knew some Greek philosophy. I have nicknamed him Mr. Philosopher.

What Did He Write?

Hebrews is an elegant sermon with an ending that is like a notation on a sticky note. The sticky note has the label

---

1. Harrington, *Who Is Jesus?* 141.

"word of exhortation" (13:22–25). Throughout this sermon, the author exhorts his tired listeners to keep going while being strengthened by faith in God and assurance of transcendent help.

What Was He Thinking?

The writer wanted to help second-generation Christians remain faithful and confident. Persecution with the possibility of bloodshed appeared to be a threat.[2] His community was becoming tired. Weariness undermines confidence. He wrote, "Do not, therefore, abandon that confidence of yours; it brings a great reward" (10:35).

Hopeful Positions

Being both a philosopher and theologian, Mr. Philosopher offered four positions to help Christians of his time and ours to carry on with faith and trust.

1. Freedom from the fear of death: Jesus shared the human condition, which includes death, and his resurrection freed those held in slavery by the fear of death (Heb 2:15).

2. Heavenly help: Because Christians have a high priest, Jesus, who knew what it is like to be a human being, they will find grace and mercy (4:14–16).

3. Connection with spiritual ancestors: Ancestors had endured with faith even though they felt like strangers on the earth (11:13–14).

---

2. *New Interpreter's Bible*, 12:9.

4. Trustworthy God: The writer reminds his readers that when God promised that Sarah would have a child, God kept that promise and therefore is trustworthy.

ARTISTIC FEATURES

Connecting the Dots

I used to think that chapter 11, which is called the faith chapter, was the most important chapter and that chapter 8, which highlights a high priest, was more suitable for high church people. Recently I have embraced the ties between chapters 8 and 11. The idea of a high priest (or dot number 1) and faith (or dot number 2) are connected. The belief in 8:1 that we have a high priest (or pastoral helper) in heaven makes it easier to have faith like the spiritual ancestors in chapter 11.

Essence of Ethics

Artists tend to look for the essence of things and ideas. In Hebrews, three things are pleasing to God. They are faith (11:5–6), worship with reverence and awe (12:28), and sharing (13:16).

Counterbalance

While the author stresses the superiority of Christ over Moses, he also holds the faith of spiritual ancestors in high regard. Considering that as Christianity developed the New Testament authors needed to take strong and often polemic stands, the affirmation of spiritual mothers and fathers in faith is noteworthy.

Words that Color the Writing

God

The author assures his readers that God speaks through the prophets (1:1) and through a Son (1:2), and through the Holy Spirit (10:15–17).

New Covenant

Christ is the mediator of the new covenant written in the heart. The new covenant is beautifully described in chapter 8.

High Priest

Christ is the eternal high priest. This concept is developed in chapters 5–10.

Once for All

Hebrews chapter 10 contains a description of Christ as a once and for all time sacrifice (10:10). As noted in the chapter on Romans, one of my college professors suggested that Christ's sacrifice on the cross means that animal sacrifices were no longer needed. Putting an end to animal sacrifices opened the way for worship as sacrifice of praise and offering of good deeds (Heb 10:24; 13:15).

Faith

Chapter 11 is very important. The author says that faith is the assurance of things hoped for, the conviction of things unseen (11:1). In a spirit of requesting an encore, he applauds the faithful people of the Old Testament, and he pictures Jesus as the model of faith.

Second Coming

The author affirms the second coming of Christ. In the meantime, a guiding principle is being hospitable to strangers, because in so doing we may have "entertained angels without knowing it" (13:2). He advises being content with modest wealth (3:5) and trusting that God is our helper (13:6).

TEXT

As a sermon, Hebrews has three parts with three main points:

1. Chapters 1–4: Jesus, as God's word, is superior to angels and to Moses.
2. Chapters 5–10: Jesus is the great high priest.
3. Chapters 11–13: Jesus is a model of faith.

Part 1

Chapter 1

God spoke through the prophets, and in Christ, God spoke through a Son.

Chapter 2

Jesus is the pioneer of salvation. He became like us, so he understands us and is therefore a merciful high priest.

Chapter 3

Moses was faithful as a servant. Jesus is faithful as a son.

Chapter 4

God promises heavenly rest.

Part 2

Chapter 5

Jesus is a great high priest appointed by God.

Chapter 6

Jesus was a forerunner on our behalf.

Chapter 7

Jesus was not a priest through biological heritage and therefore is eternal.

Chapter 8

In Jesus we have a heavenly high priest.

Chapter 9

As high priest, Jesus can be a mediator for us in the presence of God.

Chapter 10

Christ's sacrifice was "once for all" (10:10).

Part 3

Chapter 11

Faith was the power through which Old Testament heroes did their work. The author wants continuity of faith and trust.

Chapter 12

Jesus was faithful in suffering and is an example of faith and perseverance.

Chapter 13

Continue in mutual love. Be hospitable. Trust the words of Psalm 118:6 and believe that the Lord is your helper and on your side. Do not be afraid. What can anyone do to you?

ACTIVITY

Applauding Your Spiritual Ancestors in Faith

Make a list of your spiritual ancestors. They could be people in your church or another church, your family, your community, or from the Bible.

26

The Book of Revelation

God Will Wipe Away Every Tear

OVERVIEW

Who Was the Author?

A MAN NAMED JOHN wrote Revelation. He was not the same John who wrote the Letters of John or the John who wrote the Gospel. He is called John of Patmos, because he was exiled to the island of Patmos for teaching his beliefs.

Where Was He Coming From?

John had faith in God's power and he deeply internalized belief in Scripture (especially Dan 7:2–14). He drew upon the Old Testament in times of need. He had emerging insights and motivation to record the revelatory vision that he saw while "in the Spirit." This revelation was from Christ and about Christ. I believe that John of Patmos had a poetic, artistic nature and a deep yearning for grace. His personality and desire came together in his writing, which fuses visual images and poetic words.

What Did He Write?

In the form of a letter, John wrote an apocalypse in which there is a hopeful revelation of the future and the heavenly realm. His dramatic book was meant to be read aloud and circulated among the churches. Revelation is a celebration of the risen Lord.

When and Where Did He Write?

The book was written between AD 92 and 96, at the end of the reign of Emperor Domitian.[1] The small island of Patmos is sixty miles southwest of Ephesus, so John either wrote on the island or in the general area of Ephesus.

Why?

John wanted to encourage oppressed, tired people with transcendent images of victory. He did not want anyone to worship the emperor as Lord. In his experience, Christ Jesus is sovereign.

Common Mistakes

1. Spelling: There is no *s* at the end of *Revelation*.
2. Ignoring the historical situation: Revelation should not be read as a blueprint for the end of the world. The historical situation is persecution or threat of

---

1. Brown, *Introduction to the New Testament*, 774.

persecution of people who did not participate in the worship of the Roman emperor as a God. God will bring the kingdom in God's own time. We cannot know when people will honor God and live according to Jesus's ethics of love and forgiveness.

3. Calling people you do not like "the beast" or "the antichrist": Do not do it. The beast is the Roman Emperor Domitian or perhaps Nero, who some people thought did not die and would return.

Revelation and the Old Testament

John uses many images and allusions to the Old Testament without quoting from it as Matthew did. Although John refers to many passages in the Old Testament or Hebrew Scriptures, he refreshes or reworks those images. Therefore, Revelation is not his father's prayer book.

ARTISTIC FEATURES

Images and Numbers

John's favorite number is seven, as in seven seals, seven trumpets, and seven bowls. The number six is not the author's favorite number and is inferior, in his understanding, to the number seven. The label on the beast is 666 (chapter 13). Pictorial images, many of them very scary, are piled and pasted to make clear the messages that are beyond prose or even poetry.

Line

Some scholars think that Revelation proceeds in a direct line to the heavenly New Jerusalem. Others think that John keeps returning over and over to end-time scenes.[2] My solution is to see the line like the split stitch in embroidery where you make a stitch with an even number of strands and then from the back go up through the middle of the stitch. Thus you make a straight line but by going back and then ahead. (Probably not many biblical scholars sit around doing embroidery, but many people have embroidered the tree of life, which is featured in Rev 22).

Perspective

John's perspective is that through the death and resurrection of Jesus, God's victory over sin has already been achieved. Therefore when Christians are persecuted they should hold fast to their faith. The persecutors, symbolized in Revelation by the Roman emperor, will be destroyed.

Counterbalance

Despite all the pronouncements of impending punishments for those who persecuted people in the early church, there are hints of universal salvation. Those passages are 5:13, 14:6–7, 15:3–4, and 20:12.

God in Color, Light, and Silence

Sometimes the beauty of God is too deep for words. God, beyond words, is depicted in color. The one seated on the throne (God) in the throne room is described as looking like

---

2. Harrington, *Revelation*, 13–14.

jasper and carnelian. These gems suggest warm brown and reddish-orange tones. The throne is surrounded by a rainbow that looks like an emerald (4:3–4). Described through color, God is beautiful. God is also experienced as light in the temple in the New Jerusalem, where there is no need for light because the glory of God is light (21:22–26).

Silence may be deepest worship and preparation for serving. Following the worship service with people from many nations singing praises (7:9–17), the Lamb opens the seventh seal, and there is silence for about half an hour (8:1).

As an artist and poet, I treasure color, light, and silence through which I can contemplate beauty. When color, light, and silence are experienced as revealing God, then religion has an aesthetic or artistic dimension. Enjoyment of vistas of beauty and artistic expressions can be part of anyone's spirituality.

REVELATION AS DRAMA

When I was a student at Albion College, my Methodist New Testament professor said that sometimes Revelation is seen as a seven-act play. My future husband, unknown to me at the time, heard the same thing from his New Testament professor at William Jewell College, a Southern Baptist college. Taking off on that idea, I will summarize Revelation in four segments, which consist of an introduction and parts 1, 2, and 3. The main points of each part will suggest three scenes of a play.

The Book of Revelation

Introduction

Imagine a stage manager introducing the author, his book, his first assignment to write seven letters, and the motif of heavenly worship. To borrow a phrase from Paul, the stage manager is willing to be a fool for Christ (1 Cor 3:18) and is dressed in a clown suit. He wiggles his red nose and says you have already met John. In Revelation (1:4) John identifies himself as the author in a salutation, "John to the seven churches that are in Asia." In (1:9) he goes on to identify himself as "I, John, your brother."

Mr. Clown continues saying that John understands his letter as words of prophecy (1:3). He has a religious experience and vision of the risen Christ who tells him to write letters to seven churches and tell the people what they are doing wrong and what their rewards will be if they persevere. The only church that is not criticized is named *Philadelphia* (3:7–13), but, of course, everyone in that church has to keep on keeping up the faith.

In chapter 4, heavenly worship is described and people sing, "Holy, holy, holy, the Lord God the Almighty, who was and is and is to come" (4:8). Heavenly worship will continue to be a motif throughout the book. Mr. Clown waves goodbye saying, "Sad Clown, I am, and tired too, but neither tragedy nor death will win in the end." Sit back. Stay tuned and see how goodness will win intrinsic peace.

Scene 1

Imagine the stage manager, Mr. Clown, walking on stage and placing a banner into a stand with the words, "Christ with God is Ruler."

Chapter 5

The Lamb, a symbol of Christ, is deemed worthy to open the scroll because he saved the saints and made them into a kingdom of people serving God.

Chapter 6

The Lamb opens the seven seals. The fifth seal opens to show all the martyrs who have died, and so people wonder about future justice for martyred and persecuted people.

Chapter 7

The people of God are victorious, sealed, and saved out of every tribe of Israel. They are robed in white and worship God day and night.

Chapter 8

The angel breaks the seventh seal and for a while there is silence. Then seven trumpets blow and all kinds of trouble that echo Exod 7–10 plague the earth.

Chapter 9

More woes come. Even some people who escaped did not stop worshiping idols of bronze, stone, and wood.

Chapter 10

John eats a scroll that an angel gave him. It tastes sweet but turns bitter in his stomach. His message will be bittersweet. Suffering will be bitter, yet ultimate triumph will be sweet.

Chapter 11

After more woes, God's temple in heaven is laid open. John paints a picture of Christ as ruler, who has started to reign in the kingdom of God.

Scene 2

Mr. Clown walks onto the stage and places a banner with the words, "God wins in the battle of good over evil."

Chapter 12

Satan, the dragon, puts his anger into the beast, the Roman Empire. The woman clothed in the sun is multidimensional. She can stand for the people of God who make up the church or for Mary, the mother of Jesus. Her offspring are those who keep God's commandments and maintain their testimony to Jesus. In the heavenly war, Michael and his angels fight the dragon. The woman escapes on eagle wings (v. 14). The dragon goes off to fight the church.

Chapter 13

The big beast from the sea is the emperor. The beast from the land, a lesser beast, is an official of Rome who promoted worship of the emperor and the goddess Roma.

Chapter 14

The companions of the Lamb, who died because they refuse to worship idols, are saved and sing a new song. John reports his vision of the gathering of the righteous and judgment of the wicked in a metaphor of harvesting grain that is based on Joel 4:13.

Chapter 15

In a preview of the end, the theme of all nations worshiping God is the centerpiece of the book. In the hope that people will repent, angels are given seven plagues to use. Today the word *plague* suggest something like a flu epidemic, but in this book *plague* means terrible disasters.

Chapter 16

Through seven plagues, Babylon, a symbol of Rome, suffers enormous disasters.

Chapter 17

John has a vision of the great whore as a symbol of Babylon and Rome. She sits on a beast that has ten horns and seven heads (17:5–7). (Rome was built on seven hills.)

Chapter 18

Babylon falls. It was a bad day for the Roman board of trade! The economic base was in ruins. There is vindication for the people who worship God. (John wrote that Babylon fell before it did because he was so sure that it would.)

Chapter 19

God reigns. The kingdom is stronger than Rome. Christ, who is called "Faithful and True" (v. 11), charges in on a white horse like the Lone Ranger. Christ as a wise warrior is also called "King of Kings" and "Lord of Lords" (v. 16).

Scene 3

Mr. Clown places a third banner on the stage. This banner proclaims, "Peace is restored, and death does not have the last word."

Chapter 20

There is a first battle and then the first resurrection, where faithful people enjoy peace for a thousand years. Satan is released from prison and for a short time causes trouble and finally is defeated forever. Those who have died are judged according to their deeds (v. 12).

Chapter 21

Through the sustenance of symbol and the power of poetry, John of Patmos assures readers of his time and ours that death does not have the last word. "See, the home of God is among mortals. He will dwell with them; they will be his peoples, and God himself will be with them; he will wipe every tear from their eyes. Death will be no more; mourning and crying and pain will be no more, for the first things have passed away" (vv. 3–4). There is no need for a temple because God is the temple. In the New Jerusalem, there is no need of light because the glory of God is its light and its lamp is the Lamb (vv. 22–23).

Chapter 22

The angel shows John the river of the water of life and the tree of life with twelve kinds of fruit and leaves for the healing of the nations (v. 2). Jesus is the bright morning star. The Spirit and the bride invite all saying, "And let everyone who is thirsty come. Let anyone who wishes take the water of life as a gift" (v. 17). The invitation flows into a benediction, which captures a deep yearning for grace. The desire for grace is in itself a blessing.

Imagine the stage manager walking slowly on stage. Mr. Clown looks peaceful. He wipes a tear from his eye, and then he smiles. Quoting from Revelation he says, "Come, Lord Jesus! The grace of the Lord Jesus be with all the saints. Amen" (vv. 20–21).

ACTIVITIES

Images of Hope

The images of Jesus as the bright morning star (22:16) and a tree of life with leaves for the healing of the nations (22:2) are images of hope. There is hope for healing and holiness and for ongoing light and life now and forever. If you wish, you may use the tree shape at the end of the chapter, enlarge it, and paste on pictures of fruit or leaves.

Looking at Art

Edward Hicks painted many variations of his most famous theme, which is the peaceable kingdom. Sister Wendy brings us one of his paintings.[3] His painting, *The Peaceable Kingdom*, depicts chapter 11 of the Old Testament book of Isaiah. Edward Hicks wanted to represent the peace between people and animals that is depicted in Isaiah. In my sense of things, this painting also neatly matches the peaceful and harmonic conclusion in Revelation. Native Americans and American settlers are at peace together. Wild animals and children rest in the shade of a tree. I recall words in Revelation that speak of the redeemed: "They will hunger no more, and thirst no more; the sun will not strike them, nor any scorching heat" (7:16).

Furthermore, it seems to me that the restoration of the heavenly city, which is like a new Garden of Eden, echoes the peaceable kingdom theme in Isa 11. *Harper's Bible Commentary* states that the eschatological or future restoration of Eden, like the conditions that are found in Isaiah,

---

3. Beckett, *Sister Wendy's 1000 Masterpieces*, 204.

are important in apocalyptic thought.[4] In Revelation, the heavenly city is Eden restored both as a state of mind and as a sacred place.

Art Project

Using polymer compound or self-hardening clay that can be found in many craft stores, create a lion and lamb, sheep and a wolf, or another combination of animals to symbolize the peaceable kingdom and the restored Eden. Surprising friends include bear and butterfly, cat and dog, elephant and mouse, leopard and skunk, badger and bunny. Use your imagination to think of others. The tree of life could be a backdrop for the animals.

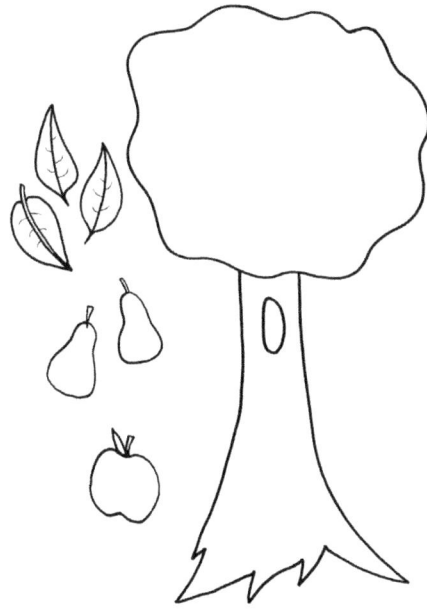

---

4. *Harper's Bible Commentary*, 1318.

Chart of New Testament Lenses

Matthew	Jesus as fulfillment of law and prophets
Mark	Cross and suffering
Luke	Prayer, compassion, concern for lost and lonely
John	Eternal love
Acts	Empowerment through the Holy Spirit
Romans	Justification by faith and assurance that nothing—including earthly powers and troubles—can separate us from the love of God
1 Corinthians	Love
2 Corinthians	New creation in Christ
Galatians	Christian freedom
Ephesians	Universal fellowship
Philippians	Christ as preexistent and suffering servant
Colossians	Unity and fullness
1 Thessalonians	Walking in holiness
2 Thessalonians	Patience

1 Timothy	Hopes on God
2 Timothy	Endurance
Titus	Sound faith and solid leadership
Philemon	Brothers and sisters in Christ
Hebrews	Christ as a high priest who helps us walk in faith
James	Christian service completing faith
1 Peter	Living as servants of God
2 Peter	Growing in grace and godliness
1 John	God as love and light
2 John	Loving one another
3 John	Imitation of good
Jude	Christian responsibility
Revelation	Triumph of good over evil; triumph of Christ over human rulers and all earthly powers and troubles

Author's Letter to Teachers

Dear Teachers,

For years I have wished that Sunday school classes could be more like college courses. That desire fueled the writing of *My First Introduction to the New Testament* and also my previously published book, *An Artistic Approach to New Testament Literature*, from which this book is derived. These two books are companion pieces. To be honest, I have a hard time knowing exactly what age groups will benefit from my books. For this book, I have landed on an optimistic estimate of ages twelve and up.

My hope is that ministers and lay teachers will use both books with adults, and in turn adults will want to use *My First Introduction to the New Testament* with middle school and high school students. Teachers of adults may find that the shorter chapters in *My First Introduction to the New Testament* can be used to summarize material in my first book. Some high school juniors and seniors will, I believe, be ready for *An Artistic Approach to New Testament Literature*. Both books will prepare young readers for college courses. Most of my readers will believe in God. However, Jesus's way is not for Christians only. Therefore I have made a modest attempt to translate some faith statements into non-theistic language.

I think that most chapters in this book can be covered in one session. Two exceptions are the chapters on Romans and Revelation, which could be taught in two sessions. Teachers may want to read each chapter to the students and then have them do an activity. Of course, there may be students who are willing to read. My suggestion is to keep homework at a minimum. Perhaps some students will want to read from the Bible in preparation or as a review, in which case my book will give a sense of what to expect.

I deeply appreciate your interest in considering, reading, teaching, and sharing my books. Thank you.

Grace and peace,

Sharon

For Further Study

Armstrong, Karen. *The Bible: A Biography*. New York: Atlantic Monthly Press, 2007.
Bainton, Roland H. *Here I Stand: A Life of Martin Luther*. Nashville, TN: Abingdon, 1978.
Beckett, Wendy, and Patricia Wright. *Sister Wendy's 1000 Masterpieces*. New York: DK Publishing, 1999.
Brown, Raymond E. *An Introduction to the New Testament*. New York: Doubleday, 1997.
Chace, Sharon R. *An Artistic Approach to New Testament Literature*. Eugene, OR: Wipf & Stock, 2008.
Duling, Dennis C., and Norman Perrin. *The New Testament: Proclamation and Parenesis, Myth and History*. Fort Worth, TX: Harcourt Brace, 1994.
Harrington, Daniel J. *The Gospel of Matthew*. Collegeville, MN: Liturgical Press, 1991.
———. *How to Read the Gospels: Answers to Common Questions*. Hyde Park, NY: New City Press, 1996.
———. *Paul's Prison Letters: Spiritual Commentaries on Paul's Letters to the Philippians, and the Colossians*. Hyde Park, NY: New City Press, 1997.
———. *Revelation: The Book of the Risen Christ*. Hyde Park, NY: New City Press, 1999.
———. *Romans: The Good News according to Paul*. Hyde Park, NY: New City Press, 1998.
———. *The Synoptic Gospels Set Free: Preaching without Anti-Judaism*. Mahwah, NJ: Paulist Press, 2009.
———. *What Are We Hoping For? New Testament Images*. Collegeville, MN: Liturgical Press, 2006.
———. *Who is Jesus? Why Is He Important? An Invitation to the New Testament*. Franklin, WI: Sheed & Ward, 1999.

Hooker, Morna D. *The Gospel according to Saint Mark*. Peabody, MA: Hendrickson Publishers, 1991.

Keck, Leander E., ed. *The New Interpreter's Bible*. 12 vols. Nashville: Abingdon, 1994–2002.

Meeks, Wayne A., et al., eds. *The HarperCollins Study Bible: New Revised Standard Version, with the Apocryphal/ Deuterocanonical Books*. New York: HarperCollins, 1993.

Phaidon Press. *The Art Book*. London: Phaidon, 1994.

Swenson, Kristin. *Bible Babel: Making Sense of the Most Talked about Book of All Time*. New York: Harper, 2010.

www.ingramcontent.com/pod-product-compliance
Lightning Source LLC
Chambersburg PA
CBHW051103160426
43193CB00010B/1295